Homemade
with Honey

Sue Doeden

the *N*orthern plate

the Northern plate

Homemade with Honey is the fifth book in the Northern Plate series, celebrating the bounty of the Upper Midwest by focusing on a single ingredient, exploring its historical uses as well as culinary applications across a range of dishes. *Rhubarb Renaissance* by Kim Ode, *Modern Maple* by Teresa Marrone, *Sweet Corn Spectacular* by Marie Porter, and *Smitten with Squash* by Amanda Kay Paa are other books in the series.

Text and book design ©2015 by the Minnesota Historical Society. All rights reserved. No part of this book may be used or reproduced in any manner whatsoever without written permission except in the case of brief quotations embodied in critical articles and reviews. For information, write to the Minnesota Historical Society Press, 345 Kellogg Blvd. W., St. Paul, MN 55102–1906.

www.mnhspress.org

The Minnesota Historical Society Press is a member of the Association of American University Presses.

Manufactured in the United States of America

10 9 8 7 6 5 4 3 2 1

∞ The paper used in this publication meets the minimum requirements of the American National Standard for Information Sciences—Permanence for Printed Library Materials, ANSI Z39.48–1984.

International Standard Book Number
ISBN: 978-0-87351-957-1 (paper)

LIBRARY OF CONGRESS CATALOGING-IN-PUBLICATION DATA
Doeden, Sue, 1952–
Homemade with honey / Sue Doeden.
    pages cm
Includes index.
Summary: "Stirred into tea or spread onto toast, honey is a familiar tableside condiment, but in *Homemade with Honey,* Sue Doeden applies this ambrosial ingredient to a wide variety of dishes. Doeden offers tips for storing honey during its unlimited shelf life and for rescuing honey that has crystallized. And she empowers home cooks to go beyond her seventy-five recipes by offering a primer on different varieties and explaining how to substitute honey for sugar."—Provided by publisher.
ISBN 978-0-87351-957-1 (paperback)
1. Cooking (Honey) I. Title.

TX767.H7D63 2015
641.6'8—dc23

2014046119

....

Homemade with Honey was designed and set in type by Cathy Spengler. The typefaces are Chaparral, TheSans, and Cochin.

Contents

Homemade with Honey

Honey—
Wholesome, Pure, and Enchanting

I watched with interest as my sister-in-law spread her morning toast with peanut butter and topped it with not the usual layer of jam or jelly but a hefty drizzle of honey. She must have noticed the inquisitive look on my face. She offered to make the same breakfast for me. The sweet, mellow taste of honey was one my palate had not often experienced. I savored each bite of the crunchy peanut butter toast concoction. My husband and I and our young son were moving from St. Paul, Minnesota, to Fargo, North Dakota, at the time, and we were living with my brother-in-law and sister-in-law for a few weeks during the transition. Peanut butter and honey on toast was my choice for breakfast every day during that stay. Little did I know that this would be the start of my honey journey.

After that delightful episode, I would occasionally purchase the thick, golden amber sticky stuff in a plastic squeeze bottle shaped like a bear. Honey made a cup of tea taste just right and was, of course, always ready to drizzle on my peanut butter toast. When my sons were pre-

schoolers, I discovered a recipe for a type of play dough made with peanut butter, honey, and powdered milk. We all had fun playing with that soft dough that smelled like peanut butter cookies and tasted good, too.

The next stop on my honey journey was the farmers market. An invisible force pulled me to a table where the sun was hitting clear glass jars of golden honey just the right way, making them glisten like large precious gems on display. It was my first encounter with a beekeeper. I was fascinated. As we visited under the bright summer sun that day, I learned about colony collapse disorder (CCD), a phenomenon in which bees mysteriously, suddenly, and completely disappear from their hives. The passionate beekeeper explained that bees were dying at such a rapid pace that she worried there may soon be a shortage of bees to pollinate the nation's commercial crops, one-third of which rely on honeybees. I realized then that, delicious as honey may be, there is more to its story than meets the eye, or the taste buds. The labor of hardworking bees affects our food supply. While bees are off foraging for nectar to feed themselves and to make honey, they are also pollinating almond trees, lemon trees, blueberry bushes, cucumber vines, onions, broccoli, carrots, avocados—all seed crops that produce food I never want to live without. I left the market with fresh knowledge from my new beekeeping friend, a renewed appreciation for bees, and a quart-size jar of honey made by local bees.

Then a conversation with a seasoned beekeeper at a spring dinner party a few years ago resulted in an unexpected opportunity. He invited me to watch as he introduced a wooden box of at least thirty thousand bees and one queen to their new home—a hive positioned on a grassy space near basswood trees across the road from his house. Wearing a baggy white jumpsuit and a headpiece with a screen covering my face for protection, I cautiously looked on as the beekeeper expertly went through the annual process of getting a buzzing bunch of bees into the hive.

Before I headed home on that cool spring evening, I dipped my finger into a frame of thick, sticky, golden honey. The honeycomb remained from the work of bees the previous summer. Sweet and delicate, the natural substance produced by honeybees melted on my tongue. That one ambrosial taste of pure, untainted honey, never touched by human hands, in its original state exactly as the bees made it, turned my love and appreciation into an obsession with what honey lovers refer to as liquid gold.

One year later, I was putting fuzzy little honeybees into my own hives with a friend who agreed to partner with me as an adventurist in bee-keeping. Me, who as a child was afraid of bugs and who still screams at the sight of a spider. Now, each time I open a hive I am mesmerized into a Zen-like state by the low hum of bees at work and the sight of the crazy little dance they do to communicate with one another. The slightly musky, sweet fragrance of the hive puts me at ease. The sight of tiny black bee legs aglow with bright pollen never ceases to amaze

me. The hardworking honeybees can fly up to fifteen miles per hour, flap their wings about eleven thousand times a minute, travel up to six miles, and collect nectar from more than a thousand flowers on each of their foraging trips, returning with pollen and nectar to the inner sanctum of a hive to make honey. It's an incredible miracle of nature.

Each time I visit my hives, I think it is indeed a miracle that I am a beekeeper in the Minnesota north woods, learning from bees and enjoying their gift of honey. Who knew it would all begin in my sister-in-law's kitchen with that first bite of peanut butter toast with a hefty drizzle of honey on top? And isn't it remarkable that Minnesota and North Dakota are at the top of the list of honey-producing states in the country? The universe was working in my favor.

PURE HONEY

The word *honey* comes from ancient Hebrew that translates as "to enchant." Since biblical times, long before sugarcane and maple syrup were discovered, honey was the first and only sweetener available to humans.

Today, honey is not just for stirring into a cup of hot tea or drizzling over a slice of toast. Americans are consuming and appreciating pure honey more than ever as they realize it is a wholesome, all-natural food with no preservatives, no added flavorings, and no added coloring. Chefs have beekeepers tending hives on the rooftops of their restaurants, and they use the honey to give depth to their vinaigrettes, marinades, and gastriques and a pronounced sweetness to desserts and cocktails. The number of backyard beekeepers is on the rise as people realize the benefits of having bees to pollinate their fruit trees, flowers, and vegetable gardens. And, if you drive along any country road in the northland, you will very likely spot wooden hives that look like file cabinets sitting in grassy fields.

Pure honey is not the same as cane or beet sugar: it is not refined. It's a natural sweetener made from the nectar of flowers. It is composed of a complex mix of naturally flavored sugars as well as trace enzymes, minerals, vitamins, and amino acids.

Look for pure honey harvested by local beekeepers. This honey has been extracted from the honeycomb by the beekeeper. Most often, it's been strained through fine mesh before being bottled. Some prefer unfiltered honey, in which you may find miniscule bee parts, pollen, and bits of wax cappings from the honeycomb suspended in the viscous golden nectar. Some of these little surprises will eventually float to the top of the honey, and some will sink to the bottom of the jar. They are totally edible, if that's the sort of thing you enjoy eating. Find local honey at farmers markets, roadside produce stands, food co-ops, specialty food shops, and health food stores. Some grocery stores carry local honey.

As you begin to collect honey, you'll notice a variety of colors. There are more than three hundred unique varieties of honey in the United States alone. The color, texture, fragrance, and taste of honey are all influenced by the types of blossoms the bees go to for nectar. You'll discover the lighter-colored honey has a milder taste. Darker honey has a more distinct, robust flavor.

Basswood honey from the beekeeper who first introduced me to a bevy of bees and their hive is pale yellow to golden, with a distinct flavor that lingers on the tongue. Someone once gave me a large container of honey from her grandfather's hive. When I took off the lid, I was greeted with the wonderful fresh aroma of apples. It was basswood honey. For an exquisite pairing with a glass of chardonnay or sauvignon blanc, drizzle basswood honey over goat cheese and serve with slices of tart apples.

Bees love clover. Depending on the variety of clover, the honey can be almost white to a light amber color with a delicate, flowery flavor. This honey is familiar to most people because it is readily available. Eat it right from a spoon for a luxurious treat.

Wildflower honey is an all-purpose honey derived from the nectar of a wide variety of blooms. The color can vary from light to dark, with a complex flavor influenced by the nectar's source.

You may need to work up to the robust, earthy, molasses-like flavor of thick, dark buckwheat honey. It can be overpowering in some dishes. It's good for mixing into barbecue sauces, and it's a perfect replacement for maple syrup on pancakes and waffles. Use it to make gingerbread.

KEEPING BEES HAPPY AND HEALTHY

You don't need to take up beekeeping to take care of bees. There are things you can easily do to protect the honeybee population. It isn't difficult to transform your yard, garden, or patio into a haven for honeybees.

- Include honeybee-friendly plants in your landscape. Nectar-producing wildflowers, including asters, goldenrod, sunflowers, and even dandelions and clover, will provide food for the hives.

- Plant an herb garden. Bees love the blossoms of mint, oregano, thyme, marjoram, and lavender. And you will love snipping fresh herbs from your garden to enjoy in your baking and cooking.

- Plant long-blooming flowers or a variety of plants that will bloom at different times throughout the spring, summer, and fall. Try to group at least ten bee plants in a bunch. The greater the plant diversity, the more bees you will attract and support. You'll also be bringing more beauty to your own surroundings. Ask at your local nursery for bee-friendly plants that grow well in your area.

- Honeybees need a place to get fresh, clean water. Fill a shallow basin, similar to a birdbath, with pebbles and add water. Float some twigs in the water, too, so that the bees have a place to land when they want a drink. Be sure to keep this water supply available throughout the bee season. The bees will depend on it.

- Buy plants that have not been treated with chemicals called neonicotinoids. Nurseries that offer untreated plants are happy to make it known by displaying that fact on signs or markers. Several European countries do not allow the use of neonicotinoids because the pesticides have been linked to massive honeybee losses.

- Avoid using chemical pesticides and fertilizers in your lawn and garden. They can be toxic to bees and are probably not the best for children and adults, either. Protect ladybugs and spiders. They will naturally keep garden pests in check.

- Do you really need all of that green, grassy front lawn? Make your sunny front yard a haven for bees by replacing all or part of the grassy area with flowering plants and vegetables.

If you are ready to set up a couple of beehives and get started on a new adventure with bees, there are resources to help.

I highly recommend finding an experienced beekeeper in your area

who is willing to act as your mentor. Spend a whole season with the bee-keeper as he tends to the bees before you start on your own.

Check to see if there is a group of local hobbyist beekeepers who meet regularly. Usually you are welcome to visit a couple of times before becoming an official member. You can join before you actually start bee-keeping. I've discovered beekeepers are the nicest people, and they love to share their passion.

Take a beekeeping class. Find offerings through your state exten-sion office, local community colleges, and universities.

Get a catalog from a beekeeping supplier and figure out how much of an investment is required to purchase everything you will need to start your new hobby. Minnesota-based Mann Lake Ltd. is a good place to start: mannlakeltd.com

Go to your local library to find books on beekeeping. A few that I have found helpful:

- C. Marina Marchese. *Honeybee: Lessons from an Accidental Beekeeper.* New York: Black Dog and Leventhal Publishers, Inc., 2009.

- Alethea Morrison. *Homegrown Honeybees: An Absolute Beginner's Guide to Beekeeping Your First Year.* North Adams, MA: Storey Pub-lishing, 2013.

- Thomas D. Seeley. *Honeybee Democracy.* Princeton, NJ: Princeton University Press. 2010.

HONEY IN THE KITCHEN

If you have a sweet tooth, you will love the fact that honey is sweeter than sugar. Pure honey not only sweetens the food it is mixed with; it adds dimension and depth of flavor. It's a secret ingredient. People will inquire about what you have in the dish to give it such wonderful flavor as they reach for a second helping.

Honey acts as an emulsifier in vinaigrettes and salad dressings, holding the oil and vinegar together.

Honey is also a humectant, a substance that either absorbs or helps other substances absorb moisture. This means baked goods made with honey tend to be moister and to stay moist and fresh tasting longer.

If you have some tried-and-true recipes that you'd like to make with honey, start by replacing a cup of sugar with ⅔ cup of honey. When you replace sugar with honey, it may be necessary to slightly reduce the amount of liquid in the recipe. I've found it may take a couple of times of experimenting with ingredient amounts before I get satisfactory results. I always reduce the temperature of the oven by 25 degrees when baking with honey to prevent overbrowning.

Honey never needs refrigeration, and it will never spoil if stored in airtight containers at room temperature. If the honey in your pantry happens to crystallize, just remove the top and place the container in a bowl or saucepan of warm water. In just minutes it will return to its thick liquid state. Since honey varies in thickness and granulation, use this same method to make thick honey pourable.

If the honey container's lid is stuck and you just can't get it off, hold the top of the container under warm running water to loosen it.

To measure honey, first lightly coat the measuring cup or spoon with cooking spray. The honey will roll right out.

As you cook and bake your way through this book, may you discover a new appreciation for honeybees, ignite a fresh affinity for honey in your heart and in your tummy, and find joy in creating food with honey to share with those you love.

Sips,
Starters,
and Snacks

For years I struggled each time I was asked to bring an appetizer to a party. What could I prepare that would be eye-appealing, easy to eat, and have everyone raving about its deliciousness? I eventually realized I could whip up an amazing appetizer in no time using Garlic Crostini as a canvas for toppings like goat cheese and make-ahead Blueberry-Plum Sauce or Baked Honey-Glazed Tomatoes and Whipped Feta.

Of course, for these and other exquisite appetizers, you'll need a jar of honey in the pantry, as all of these dishes are elevated to new heights of flavor with just a bit of natural sweetener. Honey even has its place in a good cocktail. With its subtle nuance, just a spoonful of honey enhances a Lemon Drop Martini and makes a Peach Bellini tingle your taste buds.

In this chapter, you'll discover that honey puts a fresh spin on easy-to-prepare morning wake-ups, midday noshes, party starters, and cocktails. These are some of my favorites.

HINT OF HONEY HOT MOCHA

If hot cocoa is your number-one winter warm-up, you can jazz it up by turning it into mocha. Unsweetened cocoa powder and instant coffee granules bring depth of flavor to hot milk. Evaporated milk makes the drink velvety and smooth. Honey—not too much—brings perfect balance to chocolate and coffee. The Hint of Honey Hot Mocha mixture can be cooled to room temperature and stored in a bottle in the refrigerator. Individual servings can be heated in mugs in the microwave. If you are serving several at a time, heat all of the coffee-spiked hot cocoa in a saucepan on the stove. And never, never, never think about saving calories by leaving off the dollop of whipped cream. Real whipped cream is a must for this drink. **MAKES ABOUT 5 CUPS**

....

  6 tablespoons unsweetened cocoa powder

  2 tablespoons instant coffee granules or espresso powder

⅓ cup honey

pinch salt

  1 (12-ounce) can evaporated milk

  3 cups milk

  1 teaspoon pure vanilla extract

  1 cup heavy cream

cinnamon sticks

....

In a heavy 2-quart saucepan, combine cocoa powder, instant coffee or espresso powder, honey, and salt. Gradually whisk in the evaporated milk. Place saucepan over medium heat. Continue to whisk until the cocoa powder is dissolved. Add milk and vanilla and continue to whisk until mixture is steaming. Do not boil.

In a medium bowl, beat heavy cream until soft peaks form.

To serve, pour hot mocha into individual cups. Add a cinnamon stick. Top each serving with a dollop of whipped cream.

Tips for the cook

- If a more potent cup is your pleasure, just add a generous splash of coffee-flavored liqueur.

- A mixture of equal parts confectioners' sugar and cocoa powder sprinkled over each serving adds a nice touch.

- A bottle or jar of Hint of Honey Hot Mocha makes an appreciated hostess gift when packaged with some cinnamon sticks and maybe even a couple of holiday mugs. Add directions for serving, and be sure to let the hostess know the liquid needs to be refrigerated; it will keep for 1 week. ◇

LEMON, HONEY, AND HERBS COOLER

Juicy, tart lemon slices lose their sharp edge when matched with the pine and floral fragrances of fresh rosemary and exquisite, sweet honey. The pungent flavor of fresh rosemary is quite distinctive and can easily overpower the more delicate essence of honey and lemon. One six-inch sprig is all you'll need for a gallon of cooler. Add the warm, sweet touch of mint to this blend, and you wind up with a drink that will soothe, cool, and relax with every swallow. **MAKES 12 CUPS**

12 cups water

¾ cup honey

 2 lemons, preferably organic

12 sprigs fresh mint, snipped from the top of the stems

 1 (6-inch) sprig fresh rosemary

ice cubes

extra lemon slices and mint sprigs for garnish

Heat 4 cups of the water in a saucepan over medium heat. Add honey and stir until honey is melted. Set aside.

Rinse and dry lemons. Cut both ends from lemons and discard. Slice lemons into very thin rounds. Remove and discard seeds. Place the lemon slices in the bottom of a 1-gallon pitcher or jar. Muddle the lemons with a long wooden spoon. Pour in honey water and remaining 8 cups of water.

Place mint and rosemary on work surface and bruise with a wooden spoon or a rolling pin to release the flavorful oils from the leaves. Add bruised herbs to mixture in pitcher. Stir well. Refrigerate, covered, for several hours or overnight. When ready to serve, fill glasses with ice cubes. Pour Lemon, Honey, and Herbs Cooler over the ice. Garnish each glass with a lemon slice and a sprig of mint.

Tips for the cook

- I suggest using organic lemons in this cooler. Free of chemical sprays, they are available in many grocery stores. Muddle, or gently smash, the lemons to release some of the tart juice from each slice.

- When your fresh herbs begin to bloom, freeze the flowers in ice cubes to add to summer beverages. Thyme or lemon thyme is a delicate little flower that will work well in Lemon, Honey, and Herbs Cooler. ◊

SMOOTHIES

Whirling a tablespoon of honey into your smoothie will add more than just sweet flavor. Raw honey aids in digestion and delivers vitamins B and C with each sip. I often throw tiny chia seeds into my smoothies. They are rich with omega-3 fatty acids, protein, antioxidants, and fiber.

Morning Wake-Up Call

This is my standard morning smoothie. Chia seeds and flaxseeds provide energy, protein, calcium, and omega-3 fatty acids. These essential fatty acids help maintain healthy skin and hair, benefit your cardiovascular health, and contribute to healthy brain function. I also add just a little spirulina powder. Spirulina is a type of blue-green algae that is rich in protein, vitamins, minerals, and antioxidants that can help protect cells from damage. The aroma of spirulina is a bit like seaweed. You won't even smell or taste it in the small amount used in this recipe. As you become accustomed to spirulina, you can increase the dose in your smoothie. Use a reputable brand. Add honey, fresh greens, a whole lemon, and frozen berries. It's a meal in a glass and a great way to start the day. **SERVES 1**

½ cup unsweetened cranberry juice

½ cup water

1 tablespoon chia seeds

1 tablespoon flaxseeds

1 teaspoon spirulina powder (see head note)

1 tablespoon honey

1 handful fresh greens

1 organic lemon, rinsed, ends cut off

1 cup frozen blueberries

4 frozen strawberries

....

Put juice, water, seeds, spirulina powder, honey, and fresh greens in blender. Use a sharp knife to remove seeds from lemon and cut it into small chunks. Add to blender along with frozen berries. Puree until smooth. ◊

AFTERNOON PICK-ME-UP

I fashioned this smoothie after the thick drinks I used to get at a health food store. Those smoothies always started with organic apple juice and frozen fruit; there was no dairy involved. **SERVES 1**

....

½ cup apple cider or apple juice

½ cup water

1 tablespoon chia seeds

½ banana

1 tablespoon honey

1 cup frozen mixed berries

....

Put ingredients in blender in order listed. Puree until smooth. ◊

Honey Peach Smoothie

Honey and peaches are a natural match, for breakfast or dessert. This smoothie is extra special when you can use fresh, juicy, sweet peaches. Frozen peaches fill in nicely when fresh aren't available. If you use frozen peaches, you won't need ice cubes. **SERVES 1–2**

1 (6-ounce) container peach yogurt

2 peaches, sliced

1 tablespoon raw honey

ice cubes (see head note)

Put yogurt, peaches, and honey into blender and puree. Add a few ice cubes and blend. Add more ice if you want a thicker consistency. ◇

SIMPLE HONEY SYRUP FOR COCKTAILS

Keep a small jar of this syrup in the refrigerator for up to a week. When you are expecting guests, be sure to have a good supply of Simple Honey Syrup mixed up and ready to go. The honey, dissolved in hot water, won't clump when added to a cocktail shaker filled with ice. Choose a mild honey. The flavor will definitely come through in this simple syrup.

To make the syrup, add equal parts hot water and honey to a glass measuring cup. Stir until honey is dissolved. Store in a jar in the refrigerator. ◇

CINNAMON CRUSH

For each cocktail:

Place a 3-inch cinnamon stick in a small bowl and cover with boiling water. Let sit for 20 to 30 seconds and then remove the cinnamon stick from water. Break into pieces. Fill a cocktail shaker with ice. Add the broken cinnamon stick, 1½ ounces whiskey, ½ ounce Simple Honey Syrup, and 2 ounces apple cider. Shake and strain into a rocks glass with ice. Garnish with a fresh cinnamon stick. ◇

HONEY–LEMON DROP MARTINI

For each cocktail:

Run a lemon wedge along the rim of a martini glass. Dip the moistened rim in superfine sugar. Chill the sugar-rimmed glass.

Put 5 ice cubes in a cocktail shaker. Add 1½ ounces of your favorite vodka, 1½ ounces freshly squeezed lemon juice, and ½ ounce Simple Honey Syrup. Shake it up. Pour into chilled martini glass. Garnish with a lemon twist. ◇

Peach Bellinis

Mimosas and Bloody Marys are always good cocktail choices at brunch time. But when fresh, juicy peaches are available, Bellinis are the way to go. The sweetness of the peaches will determine how much honey you will need to add. If the peaches are very sweet, start with just 1 tablespoon honey. Taste the puree and continue to add honey, a little at a time, until it's just right. Mix up the puree before your guests arrive and keep it chilled in the refrigerator. **SERVES 12**

- 4 cups peeled, chopped fresh ripe peaches (see tip)
- 2 tablespoons mild honey (see head note)
- 1 tablespoon freshly squeezed lemon juice
- 1 bottle Prosecco, chilled

Combine peaches, honey, and lemon juice in a bowl. Let sit at room temperature for 5 minutes, stirring occasionally.

Transfer mixture to blender. Whirl on medium speed until smooth, stopping once to scrape down sides. Cover and chill for 1 hour.

To serve, divide peach mixture evenly into 12 champagne flutes. Pour Prosecco over the peach mixture and stir gently. Be careful: the mixture will foam up.

Tip for the cook Peeling peaches is easy when you use a thin-skin peeler. Find them at kitchenware stores. ◇

Fresh Vegetable Spring Rolls
with Peanut-Honey Dipping Sauce

These spring rolls are a welcome delicate appetizer, a light lunch, or a healthful snack. Prepare the vegetables, mint leaves, and avocado. Set out a stack of rice paper rounds with a shallow dish of warmish water right beside the thin disks. Gather your family and friends together and have fun rolling up these colorful bundles. And don't even think about serving them without the Peanut-Honey Dipping Sauce. **MAKES 12 ROLLS**

....

   1 head romaine lettuce, leaves separated and ribs removed

2–3 carrots, cut into long matchsticks

   1 red bell pepper, seeds removed, cut into matchsticks

   8 ounces mung bean sprouts

   1 bunch fresh mint leaves

   2 avocados, ripe but firm, sliced thin

 12 round rice papers

     cooked brown rice or quinoa, optional

     Peanut-Honey Dipping Sauce *(recipe follows)*

....

Prepare vegetables, sprouts, mint leaves, and avocados and set aside.

Pour lukewarm water into a large shallow dish. One at a time, soak rice sheets in the warm water to soften, 20 to 30 seconds.

Lay a rehydrated rice sheet on work surface. Working quickly, place a lettuce leaf at the edge nearest to you, leaving about 1 inch to fold over. Place a portion of the carrots, pepper, sprouts, mint leaves, and avocado on top. Add rice or quinoa, if desired. Fold the edge nearest you over the filling, tuck in the sides, and roll up tightly. Repeat with remaining ingredients.

Place filled rolls on a plate and cover with plastic wrap so they don't dry out. Serve with Peanut-Honey Dipping Sauce.

Tip for the cook Cooked shrimp is a nice addition to these spring rolls.

PEANUT-HONEY DIPPING SAUCE

Although it looks like caramel, this is not a decadent sauce you can eat from a spoon. It is a delicious requirement for Fresh Vegetable Spring Rolls, though. You may want to make a double batch: it goes fast. Add some heat with a bit of chili paste or sriracha sauce.

....

¼ cup creamy peanut butter

3 tablespoons toasted sesame oil

1 tablespoon rice vinegar

2 teaspoons tamari or soy sauce

1 tablespoon grated fresh ginger, or to taste

2 tablespoons honey

....

Mix all ingredients in a small bowl until smooth and creamy. ⬥

Fresh Vegetable Spring Rolls with Peanut-Honey Dipping Sauce

BLUEBERRY-PLUM SAUCE
ON CHEESE-TOPPED GARLIC CROSTINI

This is a wonderful, quick-to-fix midsummer appetizer, when tiny wild blueberries are ripe for the picking and plump fresh blueberries are in the markets. I keep an extra baguette in the freezer so I'm ready whenever a celebratory text messages arrives: "Come on over for happy hour. Bring an appetizer." **SERVES 8**

2 cups fresh blueberries, rinsed

2 cups chopped fresh plums

2 tablespoons honey

1 tablespoon grated fresh ginger

1 teaspoon finely chopped fresh rosemary, basil, or thyme leaves

2 tablespoons red wine vinegar

coarse salt and freshly ground black pepper

Garlic Crostini *(recipe follows)*

goat cheese or cream cheese, softened

¼ cup pistachios, chopped

In a large skillet, combine blueberries, plums, honey, juice squeezed from grated ginger (discard the fibrous remains), fresh herbs, and vinegar. Bring to a boil, then reduce heat and allow mixture to simmer gently until plums break down, 15 to 20 minutes. Season with salt and pepper. Let cool completely before serving. Store in a tightly sealed container in the refrigerator.

Spread crostini with softened goat cheese or cream cheese. Spoon blueberry-plum sauce over the cheese. Sprinkle with chopped pistachios. Arrange on platter and serve.

Tip for the cook Just because this sauce is seasoned with fresh herbs doesn't mean it can't be used with all things sweet. Try it on ice cream, french toast, pancakes, toasted bagels, and even cheesecake.

GARLIC CROSTINI

This is my all-purpose crostini. These little toasts are best eaten the day they are made.

1 baguette

⅓ cup olive oil

2 chubby cloves garlic, minced

¼ teaspoon freshly ground black pepper

¼ teaspoon sea salt

⅛ teaspoon cayenne

....

Preheat oven to 350 degrees. Cut the baguette into ¼-inch-thick slices. Whisk the olive oil, garlic, pepper, salt, and cayenne in a small bowl. Brush each side of the bread rounds with the olive oil mixture. Arrange slices in a single layer on a baking sheet.

Bake the prepared bread rounds for 20 minutes, flipping halfway through. Remove crostini from oven when they are golden brown and crisp. Cool completely. Store in an airtight container at room temperature. ◊

Blueberry-Plum Sauce on Cheese-Topped Garlic Crostini

Baked Honey-Glazed Tomatoes and Whipped Feta Crostini

During the summer harvest, when small globes of bright red, orange, and yellow tomatoes are fresh from the vine, this is a perfect casual snack to enjoy with friends out on the deck. The slightly sweet baked honey-glazed tomatoes marry perfectly with the tart whipped feta, which can be prepared a day or two before serving. It's a match made in heaven. **SERVES 4–8**

3 ounces feta

1 ounce cream cheese

5 tablespoons extra-virgin olive oil, divided

2 tablespoons mild honey, divided

1 tablespoon freshly squeezed lemon juice

¼ teaspoon salt

1 pound cherry tomatoes

3 cloves garlic, minced

sea salt and freshly ground black pepper

Garlic Crostini (page 29)

Put feta and cream cheese in bowl of a food processor. Pulse until the mixture is blended. Add 2 tablespoons olive oil, 1 tablespoon honey, lemon juice, and ¼ teaspoon salt to the work bowl and continue to process until the mixture is smooth. Transfer to a bowl, and store, covered, in the refrigerator until serving time.

Preheat oven to 375 degrees. Slice cherry tomatoes in half. Place them cut-side up in a 13x9–inch glass baking dish, arranging them so they are touching with no space between them. Put garlic in a small bowl. Add remaining 3 tablespoons olive oil and 1 tablespoon honey. Use a fork or whisk to mix until honey is dissolved and mixture is well blended. Drizzle honey mixture over the tomatoes. Sprinkle with sea salt and freshly ground black pepper. Bake for 30 minutes.

Baked Honey-Glazed Tomatoes

To serve, spread crostini with whipped feta and top with honey-glazed tomatoes. Arrange on a platter. Or, for a more casual approach, set out a basket of crostini, the bowl of whipped feta, and the baking dish of honey-glazed tomatoes and invite guests to make their own.

Tips for the cook

- When preparing the tomatoes, measure the olive oil before the honey. The honey will roll right out of the oily spoon.

- Baked Honey-Glazed Tomatoes become dinner when you toss them with a half pound (8 ounces) of cooked angel hair pasta. Snip some basil leaves from your garden, tear them up, and add them to the dish. Grate your favorite Parmesan cheese over the top for garnish. Dinner is ready. ✧

Red Quinoa, Chickpeas, and Apples in Endive Canoes

Several years ago I had the opportunity to meet Rich Collins, president of California Endive Farms, at a conference. He was offering culinary professionals information about California-grown endive. Collins cleared up my question of how to correctly say endive. If you are referring to the sun-loving, curly-edged leaves with deep indentations, it's curly "EN-dive." When you are talking about a smooth, elongated head of tightly packed leaves, it is Belgian "ON-deev." These elongated leaves become little canoes, perfect for filling with all sorts of scrumptious mixtures that you can offer as a pick-up appetizer or plate and serve with a fork. Red quinoa, chickpeas, and apples tossed with cumin-scented, honey-sweetened orange juice is my favorite cargo for endive canoes. **MAKES 12 APPETIZERS**

....

1 cup red quinoa

1²/₃ cups water

1½ teaspoons ground cumin

½ cup orange juice

½ teaspoon salt

2 tablespoons extra-virgin olive oil

1 tablespoon honey

1 (15-ounce) can chickpeas, rinsed and drained

1 apple, cored and diced

½ cup slivered almonds, toasted and roughly chopped (see tip)

fresh Belgian endive, about 2 heads, leaves separated

....

Rinse quinoa in a fine-mesh sieve until water runs clear. Drain and transfer to a medium saucepan. Add water and bring to a boil. Reduce heat to medium low, cover, and simmer until water is absorbed, about 15 to 20 minutes. Remove from heat and set aside for 5 minutes. Uncover and fluff with a fork.

In a large bowl, whisk together cumin, orange juice, salt, olive oil, and honey. Add warm cooked quinoa and stir to coat. Add the chickpeas and gently mix. Cover and refrigerate until serving time.

At serving time, remove quinoa mixture from refrigerator. Stir in apple and almonds. Taste and adjust seasoning, if needed. Spoon quinoa mixture onto endive leaves, creating boats. Arrange on platter and serve.

Tips for the cook

- Toast slivered almonds on a baking sheet in a preheated 350-degree oven for about 8 minutes, until fragrant and just beginning to brown.

- Turn this dish into a satisfying salad by adding some chopped fresh spinach. ◇

Smoked Paprika Shrimp with Avocado-Lime Dip

Served right from the pan, this smoky shrimp cooked in a honey–white wine sauce is addictive. Be sure the shrimp are peeled before you cook them, and leave the tails on: they make a nice handle when you dunk them into the cool and refreshing Avocado-Lime Dip. **SERVES 4–6**

AVOCADO-LIME DIP

- 1 ripe avocado, mashed
- ¼ cup sour cream
- 2 tablespoons mayonnaise
- ½ teaspoon grated lime zest
- 1½ teaspoons freshly squeezed lime juice

Smoked Paprika Shrimp

SMOKED PAPRIKA SHRIMP

- 2 tablespoons olive oil
- 1 large shallot, minced
- 1 tablespoon smoked paprika (see tip)
- 1 tablespoon honey
- ⅔ cup dry white wine
- 1 pound jumbo raw shrimp, peeled and deveined, tails on
- 2 tablespoons chopped cilantro

....

Stir together dip ingredients. Set aside.

In a large skillet, heat olive oil over medium-high heat. Add shallots and paprika and cook, stirring, for 2 minutes or until the shallots just begin to turn golden brown. Add honey and wine. Stir and then bring to a boil. Boil until liquid is reduced by half. Add shrimp and stir constantly until shrimp are firm and cooked through, 4 to 5 minutes. Remove from heat. Sprinkle with cilantro.

Serve from pan, with guests helping themselves to the shrimp. Offer Avocado-Lime Dip on the side.

Tips for the cook

- Avocado-Lime Dip can also be used as a sandwich or wrap spread or as a topping for tacos. Swipe a tortilla chip across the dip—I'll bet you can't eat just one.

- Smoked paprika can be found in the spice aisle of most supermarkets. It comes in sweet or hot varieties. If you want to add some peppery heat to this shrimp dish, choose hot smoked paprika. ◊

HONEY BALSAMIC BLACK BEAN AND MANGO SALSA

My younger son brought this salsa recipe home from college. Over the years, I've added some ingredients and taken away others to create a salsa that has just the right amount of heat, fresh crunch, color, and balance of sweet and tart. And you can do the same. Feel free to customize the salsa to suit your own taste buds. Just don't leave out the honey. **MAKES 3½–4 CUPS**

- 2 tablespoons olive oil
- 2 tablespoons balsamic vinegar
- 2 tablespoons fresh lime juice
- 2 tablespoons honey
- 1 chubby clove garlic, minced
- 1 (15-ounce) can black beans, rinsed and drained
- 1 jalapeño, minced (you decide whether or not to remove the seeds)
- 1 firm, ripe mango, peeled and diced
- ½ cup finely chopped orange bell pepper
- ½ cup finely chopped yellow bell pepper
- ½ cup finely chopped red onion
- 1–2 plum tomatoes, seeds removed, diced
- 1 avocado, diced
- 2 tablespoons minced cilantro
- tortilla chips

In a small bowl, whisk together olive oil, balsamic vinegar, lime juice, honey, and garlic. Set aside.

In a large bowl, combine black beans, jalapeño, mango, orange and yellow peppers, red onion, and tomatoes. Stir in oil and vinegar mixture. Cover and refrigerate for up to 1 day. At serving time, add avocado. Sprinkle with cilantro or offer cilantro on the side. Serve with tortilla chips.

Tip for the cook Serve this salsa as a side salad with grilled chicken or beef. ◊

QUICK WAYS WITH HONEY

- On a tray, arrange fresh figs, goat cheese, and almonds with a small bowl of honey and some sliced baguette.

- Chop 1 or 2 cloves of garlic. Cook in some olive oil, stirring, until garlic just begins to turn golden brown. Immediately transfer to a plate to cool. Spread ricotta cheese in a layer about ½ inch thick on a serving platter. Drizzle with honey. Scatter garlic over the honey. Serve with toasted baguette slices. If you make your own ricotta, this is a delicious way to take advantage of its lovely flavor and creamy texture.

- Lay out one square of thawed puff pastry on your work surface. Spoon a couple of tablespoons of honey in the center of the pastry. Sprinkle with chopped nuts and dried cranberries. Place a round of

Brie cheese over the honey and nuts and dried fruit. Drizzle more honey on top of Brie and sprinkle with more nuts and dried fruit. Wrap puff pastry around the cheese as though you are wrapping a gift. Lay seam-side down on a parchment paper–lined baking sheet. Brush with a mixture of 1 egg whisked with water. Bake in preheated 350-degree oven for 30 minutes or until golden brown. Serve with apple slices, pear slices, and crostini or crackers.

Berries and Bran Muffins (page 48) >

Bread *and* Breakfast

oney is a natural sweetener that pairs perfectly with fresh fruit, dried fruit, whole wheat, seeds, nuts, and oats. That sounds like the makings of breakfast and bread to me.

Plump Sunflower White 'n' Honey Wheat Crescent Rolls created from a bowl of chilled no-knead dough will bring homey warmth to your holiday dinner table and your Sunday-night suppers. Moist and tender apricot- and walnut-studded scones come to life when they are painted with honey and are just as delicious with a cup of coffee for a midday treat as they are first thing in the morning. When you're feeling decadent, how about a thick slice of Honey-Sweetened Double Chocolate Pear Bread to start your day? Maybe you prefer a stick-to-the-ribs kind of breakfast. You'll be surprised at how sublime morning oatmeal becomes when it's gussied up with honey and baked in the oven.

Bread and breakfasts don't get any better than this.

HONEY-PAINTED APRICOT AND WALNUT SCONES

The combination of butter and cream make these rich scones a breakfast of pure decadence, especially when you sip a cup of dark roast coffee between bites. Walnuts and dried apricots are my favorite stir-ins, but I've also used pecans and dried cranberries with tasty results. The honey paint turns these scones into golden beauties. If you want to take them right over the top, just add a cup of chopped quality dark chocolate to mingle with the walnuts and apricots. You'll be so glad these scones are large! **MAKES 8 LARGE SCONES**

2 cups all-purpose flour

2½ teaspoons baking powder

½ teaspoon salt

⅛ teaspoon ground nutmeg

2 tablespoons sugar

½ cup (1 stick) cold unsalted butter, cut into ½-inch cubes

2 tablespoons honey

1 cup chopped dried apricots

1 cup coarsely chopped walnuts

1 cup heavy cream

½ cup half-and-half

HONEY PAINT

¼ cup honey

2 teaspoons sugar

....

Arrange oven racks in upper and lower thirds of oven and preheat to 425 degrees. Line 2 large baking sheets with parchment paper. Set aside.

In a large bowl, use a whisk to blend flour, baking powder, salt, nutmeg, and 2 tablespoons sugar. Add butter and 2 tablespoons honey. Use a pastry cutter or two forks to work the mixture until it looks like coarse crumbs. (Mixing the dry ingredients and cutting in the butter and honey can be done in a food processor; transfer mixture to large bowl.) Stir in apricots and walnuts. Add heavy cream and half-and-half, and stir until just combined.

Drop 4 mounds of batter, about ½ cup each, onto each of the prepared baking sheets, leaving 2 inches of space between each one.

Make the honey paint by heating ¼ cup honey (see tip). Use a pastry brush to brush half of the honey over the tops of unbaked scones. Sprinkle each with ¼ teaspoon sugar.

Bake scones for 20 to 24 minutes, switching positions of baking sheets halfway through. Scones should be puffed and golden. Allow to cool for 2 minutes on baking sheets. Brush the remaining half of the honey over each hot scone. Transfer to rack and allow to cool.

Tip for the cook Heat honey by putting it in a small jar or custard cup. Set the jar or custard cup in a pot of hot water, with just enough water to come up to the level of the honey. The honey will warm up and become a consistency that is easy to brush. ◊

SUNFLOWER WHITE 'N' HONEY WHEAT CRESCENT ROLLS

The nutty crunch of sunflower seeds tucked into these puffy crescents of yeast dough give the rolls distinct character. This recipe is perfect for the novice bread baker because the dough is refrigerated overnight and there is no kneading involved. Enjoy them fresh and fragrant from the oven with your favorite soups and stews. **MAKES 32 ROLLS**

2¼ teaspoons (1 packet) active dry yeast

1 teaspoon sugar

1 cup warm (105–10 degrees) water

½ cup (1 stick) butter, melted and cooled, plus 2 tablespoons butter, melted and cooled

⅓ cup plus 1 tablespoon honey

3 eggs, well beaten

2 cups all-purpose flour

2 cups whole wheat flour

1 teaspoon salt

¼ cup raw or roasted shelled sunflower seeds

In a large mixing bowl, dissolve yeast and sugar in the warm water. Allow to sit for a few minutes. When yeast mixture is bubbling, stir in ½ cup melted butter, ⅓ cup honey, and beaten eggs. Stir in all-purpose flour, whole wheat flour, and salt. Mix well to make a very soft dough. It will still be a bit sticky. Cover bowl tightly with plastic wrap. Refrigerate several hours or overnight.

When ready to bake, mix the remaining 1 tablespoon honey with the remaining 2 tablespoons melted butter. Set aside. Lightly grease 2 or 3 large baking sheets. Preheat oven to 375 degrees.

Remove dough from refrigerator and immediately divide into quarters. On a lightly floured surface, working with one portion of dough, roll into a circle about ¼ inch thick. Brush with melted butter and honey mixture. Sprinkle with 1 tablespoon sunflower seeds. Use a sharp knife or a pizza slicer to cut 8 pie-shaped wedges. Roll up each wedge from the wide end to the tip. Place on a greased baking sheet. Bend into crescent shapes. Repeat process with remaining three portions of dough. Cover and let rise in a warm place until doubled in size, about 1 hour. Bake until golden, 10 to 12 minutes. Transfer hot rolls to wire rack. Brush any remaining honey-butter mixture over the hot rolls. ◊

Honey-Sweetened Double Chocolate Pear Bread

Chocolate, walnuts, and pears live in perfect harmony in this not-too-sweet loaf. A hit of cinnamon adds just enough warm, woody fragrance and flavor to the chocolate batter to turn this bread into a loaf of magnificence, with morsels of chocolate hiding inside. **MAKES 1 (9X5–INCH) LOAF**

....

1	cup buttermilk
½	teaspoon baking soda
½	cup (1 stick) butter, softened
⅔	cup honey
2	eggs
1¾	cups all-purpose flour
½	cup unsweetened cocoa powder
1	teaspoon cinnamon
½	teaspoon baking powder
½	teaspoon salt
1	firm, ripe pear, peeled, cored, and diced
¼	cup semisweet chocolate mini-morsels
½	cup chopped walnuts

....

Preheat oven to 325 degrees. Grease a 9x5x3–inch loaf pan. Set aside.

Pour buttermilk into a 2-cup glass measure. Whisk in baking soda. Set aside.

In a large bowl, use an electric mixer to beat butter until creamy. Gradually add honey and beat until well blended and smooth. Add eggs, one at a time, beating after each addition. Add buttermilk and baking soda mixture and blend at low speed.

Sift flour with cocoa powder, cinnamon, baking powder, and salt. Add to butter mixture and blend at low speed. Use a spoon to fold in pear, chocolate morsels, and walnuts.

Turn batter into prepared loaf pan. Bake for 1 hour or until wooden pick inserted in center of loaf comes out clean. Cool in pan on wire rack for 15 minutes. Carefully turn loaf out of pan. Allow to cool completely on wire rack.

Tip for the cook When baked in mini-loaf pans, this bread turns into six delightful little chocolate gifts. The pans I use measure 4¼x2¼ inches on the bottom. They hold exactly 1 cup of water when filled to the very top. These little loaves take just 25 to 30 minutes to bake. ◊

Honey-Sweetened Double Chocolate Pear Bread

RICOTTA PANCAKES

Pull out your widest spatula to flip these thin, light pancakes. Top them with seasonal fruit, your favorite jam, or pure maple syrup. My favorite adornments to these rich, barely sweet rounds are thinly sliced fresh peaches or apricot fruit spread. But you'll make everyone around the table happy when you offer a topping of Honey-Baked Bananas with Pecans (page 47). **MAKES 14 (6-INCH) PANCAKES**

....

6 eggs

¼ cup canola oil (non-GMO preferred)

¼ cup half-and-half

2 tablespoons mild honey

½ teaspoon pure vanilla extract

1 cup whole milk ricotta cheese

¼ teaspoon salt

½ cup all-purpose flour

....

Put eggs, oil, half-and-half, honey, vanilla, ricotta cheese, and salt in blender. Blend for 1 minute. Add flour and blend. Batter will be thin.

Preheat nonstick griddle or pan over medium-high heat. For each pancake, pour ¼ cup batter onto griddle. As soon as bubbles begin to appear, flip with a wide spatula. Remove from griddle when underside is golden brown. If pancakes are too dark, lower the heat. Serve warm, with desired toppings. ◊

HONEY-BAKED BANANAS WITH PECANS

Try these baked bananas stirred into a bowl of hot oatmeal or spooned over premium chocolate ice cream. **SERVES 4–6**

½ cup chopped pecans

4 firm, ripe bananas

2 tablespoons butter, melted

¼ cup honey

1 tablespoon freshly squeezed orange juice

Preheat oven to 375 degrees. Arrange pecans on a rimmed baking sheet and toast in oven for 8 minutes or until fragrant. Transfer hot pecans to a plate and set aside.

Slice bananas into ½-inch-thick rounds. Arrange in a single layer in a shallow baking dish. Mix butter, honey, and orange juice. Use a pastry brush to coat the banana slices with the honey mixture. Bake for 15 minutes. Remove from oven and sprinkle with toasted pecans. Serve warm. ◇

Berries and Bran Muffins

If mention of a bran muffin elicits visions of a dry and crumbly, choke-provoking experience, these muffins will change your mind. Honey brings not only sweet balance to the earthy flavor of whole wheat flour and wheat bran but also moistness that isn't often found in bran muffins. Coconut oil provides healthful fat. When fresh berries are not in season, gently stir some frozen berries into the batter. **MAKES 18 MUFFINS**

1¼ cups all-purpose flour

1¼ cups whole wheat flour

2 cups wheat bran

2 teaspoons baking soda

½ teaspoon salt

2 eggs

⅔ cup honey

⅓ cup sugar

½ cup coconut oil, melted

2 cups buttermilk

18 fresh raspberries (see head note)

¾ cup fresh blueberries (see head note)

Preheat oven to 375 degrees. Grease 18 muffin cups with nonstick cooking spray. Set aside.

In a large mixing bowl, use a whisk to mix all-purpose flour, whole wheat flour, wheat bran, baking soda, and salt. In another bowl, use a whisk to beat eggs. Add honey and sugar and mix well to blend. Whisk in coconut oil and buttermilk. Add dry ingredients and stir just until they disappear into the batter.

Spoon batter into prepared muffin tins, filling two-thirds of the way to the top. Push a raspberry into the center of each muffin. Surround the raspberry with blueberries. Bake for 15 minutes. Allow muffins to cool in pan for 5 minutes. Carefully transfer muffins to wire rack to cool completely. ◇

CRUNCHY HONEY RHUBARB MUFFINS

These muffins are moist and not too sweet, with little bits of tart rhubarb and crunchy pecans in each bite. They are best eaten the day they are baked, when the cinnamon-spiked topping is crunchy. Once they've been held overnight in a covered container, the topping gets soft, but it doesn't lose its utterly irresistible cinnamon-spiced pecan and brown sugar flavors. Cooled muffins can be stored in the freezer for up to two weeks. Thaw at room temperature. Just before you are ready to serve, warm them in a 325-degree oven for 5 to 7 minutes. **MAKES 12 MUFFINS**

½ cup coconut oil, melted

¼ cup brown sugar

½ cup honey

1 egg

½ cup plain or vanilla yogurt

1 teaspoon pure vanilla extract

1½ cups all-purpose flour

½ teaspoon salt

½ teaspoon baking soda

1 cup finely chopped rhubarb

½ cup chopped pecans

TOPPING

¼ cup brown sugar

½ teaspoon cinnamon

¼ cup finely chopped pecans

Preheat oven to 350 degrees. Grease 12 muffin cups with nonstick cooking spray. Set aside.

In a mixing bowl, combine coconut oil, ¼ cup brown sugar, honey, egg, yogurt, and vanilla. Mix well. In another bowl, sift together flour with salt and baking soda. Stir into honey mixture, blending just until dry ingredients disappear into the batter. Gently stir in the rhubarb and ½ cup chopped pecans.

Combine topping ingredients in a small bowl.

Spoon batter into prepared muffin tins, filling three-quarters of the way to the top. Spoon 1 teaspoon of topping over the top of each muffin. Bake for about 18 to 20 minutes or until a wooden pick inserted in center comes out clean. Allow muffins to cool in pan for 5 minutes. Carefully remove muffins from tin and transfer to wire rack to cool completely.

Tip for the cook Freeze plenty of rhubarb when it's in season so you can enjoy these muffins throughout the year. Chop finely and freeze in 1 cup portions. When you are ready to make muffins, just pull 1 cup of rhubarb from the freezer and stir it right into the batter. ◈

BREAKFAST COOKIES

Cookies for breakfast? Why not? A few years ago one of my biking partners brought some hearty cookies for us to eat at the start of an early-morning, forty-mile ride. She called them breakfast cookies. I liked the idea. I've created my own version loaded with oats, nuts, flax, chia seeds, and dried cranberries. These soft, chewy disks of goodness will get you going when you're on the go—by foot or by pedal. You'll need to plan ahead when you decide to make these cookies, though: the dough needs to be refrigerated overnight before baking. **MAKES 4 DOZEN COOKIES**

1 cup (2 sticks) butter, softened
1 cup honey
½ cup brown sugar
2 eggs
1 teaspoon pure vanilla extract
1½ cups white whole wheat flour (see tip)
1 teaspoon baking soda
½ teaspoon salt
1 teaspoon cinnamon
1 cup coarsely chopped walnuts
1 cup dried cranberries
2 tablespoons chia seeds
½ cup ground flaxseeds
3 cups old-fashioned rolled oats

In a large bowl, use an electric mixer to beat butter and honey together until smooth. Add brown sugar and continue beating. Add eggs and vanilla and blend well.

In another bowl, use a whisk to mix flour, baking soda, salt, and cinnamon together. Add to bowl with butter mixture and blend on low speed.

Use a wooden spoon to mix in walnuts, cranberries, chia seeds, flax, and oats. Seal bowl tightly with plastic wrap and refrigerate at least 8 hours or overnight.

When you are ready to bake the cookies, preheat oven to 350 degrees. Line 4 baking sheets with parchment paper. Drop chilled cookie dough by heaping tablespoonfuls onto prepared baking sheets. Slightly smash the cookies with the palm of your hand. Bake for about 10 minutes. Allow cookies to cool on baking sheet for a few minutes, then slide the cookie-laden parchment paper right off the baking sheet onto a counter to cool. Store in a tightly covered container.

Tip for the cook I like to use slightly nutty-flavored white whole wheat flour for added health benefits in these cookies. You can substitute with an equal amount of all-purpose flour. ◊

Breakfast Cookies

Bit of Honey Baked Oatmeal

Right out of the oven, hot and fragrant, this baked breakfast goes way beyond a bowl of plain old oatmeal. You can mix it up the night before serving. In the morning, pop it into the oven. If you happen to have leftovers, warm them up for breakfast the next day. **SERVES 6–8**

½ cup coconut oil, melted

¾ cup honey

2 eggs

¾ cup plus 2 tablespoons dairy or nondairy milk

3 cups quick-cooking rolled oats

2½ teaspoons baking powder

¼ teaspoon baking soda

½ teaspoon salt

Preheat oven to 325 degrees. Lightly grease a 9x9–inch glass baking dish with coconut oil.

In a large mixing bowl, blend oil with honey, eggs, and milk. In another bowl, stir oats together with baking powder, baking soda, and salt. Dump oat mixture into honey mixture and stir to combine. Pour mixture into prepared baking dish. Bake for about 30 minutes. Serve hot.

Tips for the cook

- You can easily double this recipe when you are serving a large group. Bake a double batch in a 13x9–inch glass baking dish. It may take a little longer to bake.

- Add seasonal fresh fruit, nuts, or dried fruit at serving time. ◊

Honey 'n' Oats Granola

I have a large jar on my counter reserved for this granola. A stainless steel scoop resides in the jar, making for easy access to this crunchy oat mixture at breakfast time or when you just need a little snack as you pass by. Since dried fruit tends to get hard and dry when it's baked with the granola, I offer it on the side at eating time—which for me could be any time of day. **MAKES ABOUT 12 CUPS**

¾ cup coconut oil

½ cup honey

1 cup brown sugar

½ teaspoon salt

1 tablespoon pure vanilla extract

8 cups old-fashioned rolled oats

1 cup sliced almonds

½ cup ground flaxseeds

½ cup wheat germ

½ cup sesame seeds

1 teaspoon cinnamon

Preheat oven to 325 degrees. In a large saucepan set over medium heat, combine oil, honey, brown sugar, and salt. Stir until the sugar is dissolved, about 3 minutes. Remove from heat, add vanilla, and stir.

In a large bowl, combine the oats, almonds, flax, wheat germ, sesame seeds, and cinnamon. Pour the warm oil and honey mixture into the oat mixture and stir until combined.

Spread the mixture evenly on two 17x12–inch rimmed baking sheets (see tip). Bake for 20 to 25 minutes, stirring once about halfway through. When granola is deep golden brown, remove from the oven. Cool completely in pan. Store in an airtight container up to 3 weeks. ◊

QUICK WAYS WITH HONEY

- Spread peanut butter over a piece of whole grain toasted bread. Drizzle with honey. Add slices of banana for something extra special.

- Butter a slice of toasted whole grain bread. Spread with honey. Arrange thin slices of your favorite apples on top.

- Make a honey butter for waffles, pancakes, and french toast by melting ½ cup butter in a medium saucepan. Remove from heat and immediately add 1 cup honey. Stir until the honey is melted. Add 2 teaspoons cinnamon and stir to blend. Serve syrup warm. Store it in a jar in the refrigerator. Right out of the refrigerator, it's perfect for spreading on slices of whole grain toast or bagels.

- How about a little chocolate butter on your toast? Melt ½ cup semisweet chocolate morsels. Allow to cool but don't let it harden. Beat the melted chocolate with ½ cup softened butter and 2 tablespoons honey until fluffy. This is heavenly spread on slices of Honey-Sweetened Double Chocolate Pear Bread (page 44). It will be a chocolate fix with a triple whammy!

- Make a spread for toast, biscuits, bread, pancakes, and french toast by whipping together 1 cup solid coconut oil, ½ to ¾ cup raw honey, 2 teaspoons cinnamon, ½ teaspoon nutmeg, ¼ teaspoon allspice, ¼ teaspoon ground cloves, and ½ teaspoon salt. Don't overwhip, or the coconut oil will liquefy and separate from the honey. Store in a sealed jar. This spread does not need to be refrigerated.

- Honey butter is a delicious spread for yeast breads, quick breads, and muffins. Blend ½ cup well-chilled, unsalted butter, cut into chunks, with ¼ cup honey in a food processor until smooth. Serve at room temperature. To make honey pecan butter, just add ⅓ cup toasted pecans to the food processor bowl and blend with the butter and honey until smooth.

Mild Honey Apple–Butternut Squash Soup with Honey-Crisp Croutons (page 66) >

Salads, Soups, *and* Sides

S oups and salads are some of my favorite foods to invent. I can get creative and let my imagination go wild. In Mild Honey Apple–Butternut Squash Soup, squash, apples, and a turnip rounded out with flavorful seasonings and honey yield a smooth, pureed soup that can be served at an elegant dinner party or sipped from a cup in front of the fireplace on a Sunday afternoon.

Fresh, seasonal ingredients combined with a honey-sweetened vinaigrette make the liveliest salads. When tossed with Spiced Honey Walnuts, roasted beets, and fruit, a bowl of greens becomes spectacular. And with honey in the house, a side of vegetables no longer needs to be boring. Honey heightens the rich flavor of broccoli roasted with garlic and balances the heat of red pepper flakes. And baked grated carrots will become a side your family regularly requests.

Soon you will be creating your own soups, salads, and sides with new ingredients combined with the sweet taste of honey.

BEET AND CARROT SALAD WITH HONEY BALSAMIC DRESSING

Raw beets? I say yes. If you've not had the opportunity to eat uncooked beets, you must try this recipe. I convinced my beet-challenged husband, who stays as far away from the earthy root as he can, to take a taste of this salad. And he kept eating it. Toss a grated beet with grated carrot—another sweet root—add a light vinaigrette, and magic happens. Even people who thought they didn't care for beets will find they just can't stop eating this unique mixture. SERVES 2–3

....

2 medium carrots

1 large red beet

1 chubby clove garlic, minced

1 tablespoon extra-virgin olive oil

2 teaspoons freshly squeezed lemon juice

1 tablespoon balsamic vinegar

red pepper flakes, to taste

1–1½ tablespoons honey

kosher salt and freshly ground black pepper, to taste

fresh greens of your choice

2–3 tablespoons sesame seeds

....

Trim, peel, and grate the carrots and beet (see tip). You can use a food processor with a grater attachment or a box grater. Ideally, you will have equal amounts of grated beets and carrots, about 1 to 1½ cups of each. Toss them together in a glass bowl.

Assemble the dressing by whisking together the garlic, extra-virgin olive oil, lemon juice, vinegar, red pepper flakes, honey, salt, and pepper. Pour the dressing onto the vegetables and mix well. Allow to sit for at least a half hour so the flavors can develop.

At serving time, spoon the salad over some fresh greens. Sprinkle with sesame seeds. Serve chilled or at room temperature.

Tips for the cook

- Use a vegetable peeler to peel the beets. Wear plastic gloves to protect your hands from getting stained. Wear an apron or an old shirt!

- This salad is the perfect canvas for a sprinkle of chopped walnuts and a few small knobs of creamy goat cheese all over a bed of arugula or curly endive. ◊

Hearty Wild Rice Salad

Full of nutty wild rice and beans, Hearty Wild Rice Salad can be served at room temperature, making it the perfect dish to take to potluck dinners and picnics under the sun. Once the wild rice is cooked, the salad quickly comes together with very little chopping involved. Seasoned with ground cumin and curry powder, this salad whispers a hint of Morocco. **SERVES 6 AS A MAIN DISH**

- 1 cup wild rice, rinsed and drained
- ½ teaspoon salt
- 3 cups water
- 2–3 cups diced winter squash
- ½ cup plus 1 tablespoon extra-virgin olive oil
- salt and freshly ground black pepper
- 2 tablespoons freshly squeezed lemon juice
- 2 tablespoons red wine vinegar
- 2 tablespoons Dijon mustard
- 1 tablespoon honey
- 1 tablespoon ground cumin
- 1 teaspoon sweet curry powder
- ¼ teaspoon Hungarian sweet paprika
- ⅛ teaspoon cayenne
- 2 cloves garlic, minced
- 1 (15-ounce) can chickpeas, rinsed and drained
- 1 (15-ounce) can red beans, rinsed and drained
- 1 (8-ounce) can water chestnuts, drained and chopped
- ½ cup sliced green onions
- ¼ cup dried cranberries, chopped

Put rice, ½ teaspoon salt, and water into a medium-sized pot and bring to a boil. Reduce heat to a simmer. Cover and cook for about 30 to 40 minutes. Rice should be tender, not mushy. Drain rice and return to pot. Keep covered while preparing ingredients for salad.

Preheat oven to 400 degrees. Put squash in an ovenproof skillet large enough to accommodate the squash in one layer. Drizzle with 1 tablespoon olive oil and sprinkle with some salt and pepper. Roast in oven for 20 to 30 minutes, until tender when poked with a fork. Remove from oven and set aside.

Make the dressing by whisking together the lemon juice, red wine vinegar, Dijon mustard, honey, cumin, curry powder, paprika, cayenne, and garlic. Gradually add the remaining ½ cup olive oil, and continue to whisk until well blended.

Put wild rice into a large glass mixing bowl. Drizzle a little of the dressing over the rice and stir to coat. Set remaining dressing aside.

Add chickpeas, red beans, water chestnuts, green onions, and cranberries, and mix with a wooden spoon. Gently fold in roasted squash. Add more dressing to taste. Season to taste with salt and pepper. Serve, or store salad in a covered bowl in refrigerator and then allow the salad to come to room temperature before serving.

Tip for the cook When you can find crunchy jicama in the produce department of your favorite grocery store, bring it home, peel it, chop it up or grate it, and use in this salad to replace the water chestnuts. ◊

FARMERS MARKET COUSCOUS SALAD
WITH SPICY HONEY VINAIGRETTE

Israeli couscous, sometimes called pearl couscous, is made of semolina and wheat flour. It's twice as big as the familiar tiny yellow semolina-based North African couscous and is toasted rather than dried. Its nutty flavor and sturdy composition gives it a chewy bite, perfect for salads. Stop by your local farmers market and load your market bag with fresh produce. Then go home, cook up some Israeli couscous in less than 10 minutes, chop up your vegetables, and you'll have this salad for lunch in no time. **SERVES 6**

VINAIGRETTE

½ cup grapeseed oil (see tip)

¼ cup honey

¼ cup Asian chili garlic sauce

3 tablespoons balsamic vinegar

2 teaspoons Worcestershire sauce

SALAD

1½ cups water

1½ cups Israeli couscous

2 large red tomatoes, diced

1 (5-ounce) bag baby spinach leaves, stems removed, coarsely chopped

1 cup diced red onion

1 cup diced cucumber

½ cup each diced green bell pepper, red bell pepper, and yellow bell pepper

¼ cup pine nuts, toasted

6 ounces feta cheese, crumbled, optional

sea salt and freshly ground black pepper

Put grapeseed oil, honey, Asian chili garlic sauce, vinegar, and Worcestershire sauce in a small bowl or pitcher and whisk to blend well. Set aside.

Put water in a medium saucepan over high heat. Bring to a boil, stir in couscous, cover, and reduce heat to low. Cook for 8 minutes. There should be no water left in the pan. Remove from heat and dump couscous into a large bowl. Pour 2 tablespoons of the vinaigrette over the hot couscous and stir to coat. Let cool to room temperature.

Add tomatoes, spinach, red onion, cucumber, peppers, pine nuts, and feta (if using), tossing to combine. Drizzle vinaigrette over top and toss gently to coat. Season with salt and pepper to taste. Serve at room temperature or chilled. Store any remaining vinaigrette in a tightly sealed jar in the refrigerator.

Tip for the cook Grapeseed oil is light and delicate with a slightly nutty flavor, which makes it a nice choice for this vinaigrette. It also has health benefits as an excellent source of vitamin E, an important antioxidant. Its high smoke point makes it a versatile oil to have in your kitchen. ◇

Mixed Greens with Roasted Beets, Spiced Honey Walnuts, and Shallot Vinaigrette

This exquisite blend of flavors and textures is a treat for those who love beets, and even for those who don't. A light shallot vinaigrette and walnuts spiced with a balanced blend of chili powder, cumin, and cayenne make this a salad to remember. You'll have more than enough of the walnuts. Refrigerate what's left of the sweet and spicy nuts. They make an irresistible pop-in-the-mouth snack! **SERVES 6**

SHALLOT VINAIGRETTE

¼ cup freshly squeezed lemon juice

2 tablespoons olive oil

2 tablespoons honey

⅓ cup chopped shallots

1 chubby clove garlic, chopped

¼ teaspoon salt

¼ teaspoon freshly ground black pepper

SPICED HONEY WALNUTS

1 tablespoon butter

¼ cup honey

1 teaspoon salt

1 teaspoon ground cumin

1 teaspoon chili powder

¼ teaspoon cayenne

2 teaspoons sesame seeds

3 cups walnut halves and pieces

SALAD

2–3 medium-sized beets

1 (4- to 5-ounce) bag mixed baby greens

2 cups baby arugula

⅓ cup dried cranberries

1 green apple, cut into matchsticks

4 ounces blue cheese, crumbled

....

Make shallot vinaigrette by putting all of the ingredients in a blender and processing until emulsified. Adjust seasonings to taste. Set aside.

For the salad, preheat oven to 400 degrees. Trim beets and wrap individually in aluminum foil. Place in a shallow baking dish. Roast for about an hour or until a sharp paring knife can easily be poked into the beets. Remove from oven and allow to cool slightly. When cool enough to handle, use your fingers or a paring knife to remove the skin from the beets. Cut beets into ½-inch cubes and set aside.

For the walnuts, line a jelly roll pan with aluminum foil and coat with butter or coconut oil. In a medium-sized saucepan, melt butter with honey over medium-low heat. Stir and cook until mixture bubbles and begins to foam. Remove from heat and add the salt, cumin, chili powder, cayenne, and sesame seeds. Mix well. Add the walnuts and stir to coat. Spread nuts in a single layer on the prepared pan. Bake at 400 degrees until lightly browned, 6 to 8 minutes, stirring once. Remove from oven and cool in pan.

To assemble the salad, place rinsed greens in a large salad bowl with cranberries and apples. Toss with just enough vinaigrette to coat the greens and make them glisten. Add beets, blue cheese, and walnuts, and toss lightly. The beets will turn everything red if you get too carried away. Serve.

See tips on page 66.

>>

Tips for the cook

- A day or two before assembling the salad, beets can be roasted, vinaigrette can be prepared and stored in a covered jar in the refrigerator, and walnuts can be made and stored in a sealed container in the refrigerator. Hide the spiced honey walnuts in the back or they may disappear by the time you make your salad.

- This salad looks beautiful when you plate it before serving. Toss the greens with cranberries, beets, and vinaigrette. Arrange the mixture on salad plates. Sprinkle with blue cheese crumbles and spiced honey walnuts. Place a small mound of apple matchsticks in the center of each salad. ◇

MILD HONEY APPLE–BUTTERNUT SQUASH SOUP WITH HONEY-CRISP CROUTONS

This creamy, tangerine-hued soup is full of surprises. Apples, sweet root vegetables, and lightly sweet and nutty butternut squash are highlighted with the addition of honey. Flavored with nutmeg, rosemary, and sage, a small shallow bowl of this soup is a beautifully rich beginning to a meal. It's also satisfying on its own with some homemade rolls to swipe up the last creamy remains. **MAKES 12 (1-CUP) SERVINGS**

2	medium leeks
3	tablespoons butter
1	medium onion, chopped
½	cup chopped celery
½	cup chopped carrot
1	pound butternut squash, peeled, seeded, and chopped
1	small turnip, peeled and chopped
2	large Granny Smith apples, peeled, cored, and chopped
¼	cup honey

4 cups vegetable or chicken broth

1 cup apple cider

¼ teaspoon ground nutmeg

¼ teaspoon dried whole rosemary leaves, crushed

¼ teaspoon dried sage leaves, crushed

½ teaspoon salt

¼ teaspoon ground white pepper

½ cup (2 ounces) shredded Gruyère cheese,
plus more for serving

½ cup heavy cream

Honey-Crisp Croutons (page 68)

....

Remove roots, tough outer leaves, and tough dark green tops from leeks. Cut leeks in half lengthwise. Fan open the leek halves as you hold them under cool running water to rinse away any dirt that may be hiding between the layers. Slice the leek halves crosswise and then chop.

In a 4-quart pot over medium heat, melt butter and cook leeks, onion, celery, and carrots, stirring often, until vegetables are tender, about 8 minutes. Add squash, turnip, apples, and honey to the pot. Cook, stirring, for another 5 minutes. Add broth and bring mixture to a boil. Reduce heat and simmer, covered, for about 45 minutes or until vegetables are tender.

Working in batches, puree soup mixture in a blender until smooth. Pour pureed soup back into the pot. Add apple cider, nutmeg, rosemary, sage, salt, and white pepper and stir well. Simmer soup, uncovered, for 10 minutes or until thoroughly heated. Add shredded cheese and heavy cream, stirring until cheese melts. Ladle soup into individual bowls. Garnish with Honey-Crisp Croutons and shredded Gruyère cheese.

>>

....

HONEY-CRISP CROUTONS

These crunchy croutons are not just for soup. Sprinkle them over a salad of fresh greens for a new taste treat.

4 pieces whole grain bread, cut into ½-inch cubes

1 tablespoon butter

2 tablespoons superfine sugar (see tip)

1 tablespoon plus 1 teaspoon honey

1 tablespoon heavy cream

½ teaspoon chili powder

¼ teaspoon smoked paprika

¼ teaspoon cayenne

¼ teaspoon salt

....

Preheat oven to 300 degrees. Spread bread cubes in a single layer on a large baking sheet. Bake for 15 minutes.

While bread cubes are toasting, melt butter in a small saucepan. Add sugar and stir to dissolve. Remove from heat. Add honey and stir until melted. Add heavy cream, chili powder, paprika, cayenne, and salt. Stir to mix well.

Pour honey mixture into a large glass bowl. Add toasted bread cubes and mix well to coat. Arrange the coated bread cubes on the baking sheet. Bake for another 15 to 20 minutes, stirring halfway through. When croutons are crispy, remove from oven and allow to cool. Store cooled croutons in a tightly sealed container.

Tip for the cook Superfine sugar, sometimes called caster sugar, can be found in well-stocked grocery stores. You can make your own by whirling some sugar in your blender. Be careful to stop before it turns to powder. ◊

QUINOA WITH BUTTERNUT SQUASH AND RED BELL PEPPER

Quinoa, an excellent plant-based source of protein, takes relatively little time to cook. Dotted with creamy butternut squash, this dish is an ideal entrée for your Meatless Monday supper alongside a tossed salad of fresh greens. It's also delicious with chicken or pork. **SERVES 4**

....

1 tablespoon coconut oil

2 cups peeled and coarsely chopped butternut squash

1 cup chopped red bell pepper

1 cup finely chopped onion

1 jalapeño, seeded and minced

2 cloves garlic, minced

1⅓ cups vegetable or chicken broth

1 cup quinoa, rinsed

2 tablespoons honey

salt

1½ tablespoons thinly sliced green onions

....

Heat coconut oil in large saucepan over medium-high heat. Add squash, red bell pepper, onion, jalapeño, and garlic. Cook, stirring, for 4 minutes. Stir in broth and quinoa and bring to a boil. Cover, reduce heat, and simmer 15 to 20 minutes or until liquid is absorbed and squash is tender when poked with a fork. Stir in honey. Taste and season with salt, if necessary. Sprinkle with green onions and serve. ◇

Sweet Pepper Wild Rice and Orzo Pilaf

Wild rice finds an unlikely partner with orzo, a rice-shaped pasta, but it's a match that works. This side dish goes well with everything. It's especially delicious with salmon and steak. Oh, and chicken, too. You'll find yourself making this pilaf often. **SERVES 6 GENEROUSLY**

1 cup wild rice

½ cup orzo

2 tablespoons butter

1 medium onion, chopped

⅔ cup chopped red bell pepper

⅔ cup chopped orange bell pepper

⅔ cup chopped yellow bell pepper

2 cloves garlic, minced

2 tablespoons honey

1 tablespoon chopped fresh flat-leaf parsley
or 1 teaspoon dried parsley

2 teaspoons soy sauce or tamari

2 teaspoons freshly squeezed lemon juice

salt and freshly ground black pepper

Rinse wild rice and put in saucepan with 3 cups water. Bring to a boil, reduce heat, and simmer, covered, until rice is done, 45–50 minutes. Kernels of rice will be split open, revealing the white inside. It should be tender but still a bit chewy. Drain and set aside.

While rice is cooking, bring 3 cups of water to a boil in a saucepan. Add orzo and cook until just tender, 8 or 9 minutes. Drain and set aside.

In a large pan, melt butter over medium heat and add onion and bell peppers, stirring to cook. When tender, add garlic and cook, stirring, for another minute. Stir in honey. Add parsley, soy sauce, and lemon juice, and stir to blend. Add cooked wild rice and orzo, continuing to stir until heated through. Season to taste with salt and pepper. Serve immediately.

Tip for the cook To reduce prep time, cook the wild rice a day or two ahead of time and store in a tightly sealed container in the refrigerator. ◊

AUTUMN RICE ON THE WILD SIDE

The nutty flavor of wild rice pairs well with squash and sweet potatoes, so why not cook them all together? This one-pot dish starts on the stove and finishes in the oven. It's a wonderful accompaniment to Thanksgiving turkey as well as pork and chicken. This side dish can become a meatless entrée with the addition of beans. Rinse and drain a can or two of pinto beans or red beans and add them to the pot along with the cranberries. If you have some Autumn Rice on the Wild Side left in the pot, make another meal out of it by mixing it with some broth and turning it into a hearty soup. This dish is versatile, easy to prepare, nutritious, and delicious. **SERVES 8 AS A SIDE DISH**

½ cup (1 stick) butter

1 cup wild rice

1 cup finely chopped onion

1½ cups orange juice

1½ cups chicken or vegetable broth

2 cloves garlic, minced

¼ cup honey

¾ teaspoon salt

¼ teaspoon ground coriander

¼ teaspoon ground cardamom

⅛ teaspoon ground nutmeg

2 cups peeled and diced sweet potatoes (about 1 pound)

2 cups peeled and diced butternut squash (about 1 pound)

½ cup chopped fresh cranberries

½ cup toasted pecan halves (see tip)

Preheat oven to 350 degrees. Melt butter in a heavy 3-quart Dutch oven. When butter is melted and hot, add wild rice and onions. Cook, stirring, for 5 minutes. While rice and onions are cooking, bring orange juice and broth to a boil. You can do this in a 4-cup glass measure in the microwave oven or in a saucepan on the stove. Add garlic to wild rice mixture and cook for 2 more minutes. Stir in honey and blend well. Add hot liquid mixture to the rice pot along with salt, coriander, cardamom, and nutmeg. Stir in the sweet potatoes, squash, and cranberries. Bake, covered, for 45 minutes, until rice and squash are tender and almost all of the liquid has cooked away. Sprinkle with toasted pecans and serve.

Tips for the cook

- Some grocery stores and natural food stores offer spices in their bulk food departments, allowing shoppers to buy spices such as coriander and cardamom, which may be used only occasionally, in small quantities rather than a whole jar. Purchasing small amounts of spices ensures fresh flavor.

- Toast pecans in a single layer on a baking sheet in a 350-degree oven for 8 to 10 minutes. I toast a pound of pecan halves at a time. If you use them regularly, store them in a sealed jar in your pantry. If you use them only occasionally, store them in the refrigerator or freezer to preserve freshness. ◇

Hot and Sweet Roasted Broccoli

It seems every family has one person who wrinkles his nose at broccoli. If you can persuade him to take just one taste of this honey-glazed, caramelized broccoli with a kick of heat, he will be popping pieces into his mouth like candy. It's addictive. Serve it as a side. Share it as a snack. Or just gobble up the whole thing by yourself. **SERVES 4**

....

1¼ pounds broccoli, cut into florets

5 tablespoons olive oil, divided

salt and freshly ground black pepper

1 tablespoon honey

4 cloves garlic, minced

½ teaspoon red pepper flakes, crushed (see tip)

....

Preheat oven to 450 degrees. In a large bowl, toss broccoli florets with 3 tablespoons olive oil. Arrange broccoli in a single layer on a rimmed 15½x10½–inch baking pan. Sprinkle with salt and pepper. Bake for 10 minutes. While broccoli is baking, mix remaining 2 tablespoons olive oil with honey, garlic, and red pepper flakes.

After 10 minutes in the oven, drizzle broccoli with oil and honey mixture. Stir to coat the broccoli. Continue baking for another 10 minutes. Broccoli should be brown and caramelized. Season to taste with more salt and pepper. Serve immediately.

Tip for the cook Adjust the amount of red pepper flakes to suit your heat tolerance. I use a full teaspoon. ◇

Elegant Baked Carrots

Carrots, simply shredded, sweetened with honey, and bathed in butter, become an elegant side dish when brought to the table in a casserole dish directly from the oven. These carrots pair nicely with any kind of meat or fish.

SERVES 4–6

1 pound carrots

1 tablespoon honey

4 tablespoons (½ stick) butter, melted

1 teaspoon salt

freshly ground black pepper

Preheat oven to 350 degrees. Use a little of the melted butter to coat the inside of a 1-quart glass baking dish. Coarsely shred carrots into a large bowl. In a small bowl, mix honey with melted butter, salt, and some freshly ground black pepper. Pour over carrots and toss to coat. Transfer carrots to prepared dish. Cover and bake 45 minutes or until carrots are tender. ◈

QUICK WAYS WITH HONEY

- In a skillet over medium-high heat, warm chunks of cooked beets in butter, stirring often. Stir in some honey, just enough to take the edge off the earthiness of the beets. When beets are heated through, remove skillet from burner. Stir in a dollop of sour cream and sprinkle with fresh dill leaves.

- Spoon a dollop of chilled Simple Honey Syrup (page 23) in the center of squash halves and sprinkle with coarsely chopped pecans during the last 10 to 15 minutes of baking time.

- Drizzle honey over servings of any kind of hot squash soup and sprinkle with minced fresh thyme or rosemary leaves.

Glazed Honey-Mustard
Pork Tenderloin Sliders (page 86) >

The Main
Event

J ust as fresh ingredients change with the seasons, so do my food desires. During the cold winter months, I look forward to re-laxed Sunday lunches of Ratatouille and Rice, a meatless dish that warms me up in no time. At the height of summer's farmers market season, a stir-fry dish glazed with honey-sweetened brown sauce is bright with colorful peppers and broccoli and makes a satisfying meal in just minutes without heating up your kitchen. Peruvian Steak Salad will have you firing up the grill for beef and vegetables that get tossed with crisp romaine lettuce. And potatoes? Yes. Baked potato wedges figure into this unique salad.

You'll discover that just a bit of honey makes a huge difference in the flavor of many entrée dishes. Whether it crisps up Honey-Kissed Fried Fish, helps brine a turkey breast, is drizzled on a spicy Jalapeño Turkey Burger, or dresses wild rice, you'll want local honey in your pantry at all times. I guarantee it.

HONEY-SOY CHICKEN KABOBS

During summer grilling season, nothing could be more colorful or convenient than kabobs. Fire up the grill and thread honey-and-soy-marinated chicken on skewers with some peppers, onions, and fresh pineapple, all brushed with a honey glaze. **SERVES 6**

½ cup soy sauce or tamari

⅓ cup honey

2 cloves garlic, minced

2 teaspoons grated fresh ginger

¼ cup freshly squeezed orange juice

5 boneless, skinless chicken breast halves (about 2½ pounds)

2 green bell peppers, cut into 1-inch pieces

2 red bell peppers, cut into 1-inch pieces

1 large onion, cut into 1-inch chunks

1 fresh pineapple, cut into chunks

....

Combine soy sauce, honey, garlic, ginger, and orange juice in a 2-cup glass measure or a small mixing bowl. Set aside.

Slice chicken breast halves lengthwise into 1-inch-wide strips. Place chicken strips in a large plastic zip-top bag. Reserve ¼ cup of the soy-honey mixture, and pour remaining marinade over the chicken. Seal bag, place in a shallow dish, and refrigerate for 1 hour, turning occasionally.

Prepare grill. Remove chicken from marinade, discarding marinade. Thread chicken, accordion style, on metal skewers. Use separate skewers for green peppers, red peppers, onions, and pineapple.

Grill skewers of chicken, peppers, onions, and pineapple over medium-hot coals for 15 minutes or until done, basting chicken frequently with reserved marinade. ◊

Honey-Soy Chicken Kabobs

MARINATED CHICKEN AND HONEYED WILD RICE

Chicken marinated in a mixture of olive oil and white wine with fresh garlic and herbs becomes succulent as it cooks slowly on the grill. Wild rice gets tossed with a sauce made sweet with honey and tart with Dijon mustard and white wine vinegar. I like making this meal with a chicken from a local farmer, wild rice harvested from the river on which I live, and honey made by my own bees. **SERVES 4**

½ cup plus 2 tablespoons white wine, divided

½ cup extra-virgin olive oil

2 tablespoons chopped fresh parsley

1 teaspoon minced fresh rosemary leaves

2 teaspoons minced garlic

½ teaspoon salt

½ teaspoon freshly ground black pepper

1 chicken, about 3 to 4 pounds, cut up

1 cup wild rice

3 cups water

2 tablespoons white wine vinegar

1 tablespoon Dijon mustard

3 tablespoons honey, divided

Early in the day, make marinade for chicken by combining ½ cup white wine, olive oil, parsley, rosemary, garlic, salt, and pepper in a small mixing bowl or 2-cup glass measure. Place chicken pieces in a large glass baking dish. Pour marinade over the chicken, turning the pieces to be sure they are coated with liquid. Cover the dish and refrigerate for 6 to 8 hours.

When it's time to start preparing the meal, remove chicken from refrigerator and allow to sit at room temperature for up to 20 minutes while you heat the grill.

Remove chicken pieces from the marinade; discard marinade. Place pieces on prepared grill and cook chicken over relatively low heat. Be patient: the cooking can take around 50 minutes. Turn the chicken halfway through cooking time.

Once chicken is on the grill, place wild rice and water in a saucepan over high heat and cover. Bring to a boil, reduce heat to low, and simmer for about 40 minutes. Make the sauce by combining remaining 2 tablespoons white wine, white wine vinegar, Dijon mustard, and 1 tablespoon honey. When rice is cooked to desired doneness, drain any remaining liquid. Stir sauce into rice gradually, adding just enough to coat the rice.

Heat remaining 2 tablespoons honey and brush over the top side of each piece of chicken during the last 5 to 10 minutes on the grill.

Spread rice on a serving platter and arrange grilled chicken over the rice. Serve.

Tip for the cook When it's too cold to be outside grilling, bake the chicken in the oven. Preheat oven to 400 degrees. Arrange marinated chicken, skin-side up, in a single layer on a rimmed baking sheet, leaving space between the pieces. Bake for 30 minutes. Brush chicken with honey, reduce heat to 350 degrees, and continue to bake an additional 10 to 30 minutes, until juices run clear when poked with a sharp knife or until an instant-read thermometer shows internal temperature of breasts at 165 degrees and thighs at 170 degrees. ◊

Spicy Honeyed Jalapeño Turkey Burgers

Ground turkey, flavored with salsa, fresh cilantro, and cumin, forms the ideal base for a spicy-sweet honeyed jalapeño topper. A little oil added to the lean meat prevents it from crumbling on the grill. I prefer the high-quality ground turkey from Kadejan, a family-run operation in Glenwood, Minnesota. It's available in food co-ops and high-end grocery stores throughout the state. **SERVES 4**

1¼ pounds lean ground turkey

¼ cup chunky salsa

¼ cup chopped cilantro

3 tablespoons canola oil (organic, non-GMO is best)

1–2 teaspoons sauce from can of chipotle peppers in adobo sauce

1 teaspoon ground cumin

1 teaspoon salt

½ teaspoon freshly ground black pepper

4 jalapeños

4 hamburger buns, sliced in half

2 tablespoons honey

1 avocado, sliced

4 slices fresh tomato

2 tablespoons sour cream

4 lettuce leaves

In a large glass bowl, mix ground turkey with salsa, cilantro, oil, adobo sauce, cumin, salt, and pepper. Shape turkey mixture into 4 patties. Place the patties on a platter, cover with plastic wrap, and place in freezer while you get the coals ready. If you're using a gas grill, keep the patties in the freezer for 30 minutes before grilling.

Slice each jalapeño in half lengthwise, leaving seeds and membrane intact. Coat each half lightly with some oil.

Place burger patties and jalapeño halves skin-side down on grill over medium-high heat. Cook burgers until they have reached desired doneness. When jalapeño skins have blistered, remove from grill. Just before burgers are done, toast the buns on the grill.

Place cooked burgers on buns. Top each with two jalapeño halves, a drizzle of honey, avocado slices, a tomato slice, a dollop of sour cream, and a lettuce leaf.

Tip for the cook I seldom use a whole can of chipotle in adobo sauce at one time. What I don't use, I simply pour into a jar and freeze. When I need some of it, I scrape the frozen mixture out with a spoon. ◇

HONEY-BRINED TURKEY BREAST

Brining is an age-old method of preserving and flavoring food. A brine—simply liquid infused with salt—has the power to season meat and poultry right down to the bone. Plan ahead, though. You'll want the turkey to take a nice long one- or two-day soak in the brine before cooking. In Honey-Brined Turkey Breast, apple juice or cider is the liquid. Honey adds sweetness as well as creating a beautiful mahogany glaze as the turkey roasts. Whether prepared in the oven or on the grill (see tip), this turkey turns out moist and juicy, with just the right balance of succulent sweet-spicy-salty flavors. **SERVES 6–8**

- 4 cups apple juice or cider
- ½ cup honey
- ¼ cup coarse kosher salt (see tip)
- 1 tablespoon Dijon mustard
- ¾ teaspoon red pepper flakes
- 1 bone-in, skin-on turkey breast half (1½–2½ pounds)
- olive oil
- 2 ribs celery, halved
- 1 apple, cut into wedges
- 2 sprigs fresh rosemary

For the brine, bring the apple cider to a boil in a 2-quart pot over high heat. Pour the hot cider into a nonreactive container that is just large enough to hold the turkey breast and the brine; an enamel, glass, or crockery bowl works best. Let cool for 5 minutes. Add the honey, salt, mustard, and red pepper flakes. Whisk until the honey dissolves. Let the brine cool to room temperature, then refrigerate until well chilled.

Add the turkey breast to the chilled brine. Weight with a plate if necessary to keep the turkey breast completely submerged. Refrigerate for 1 to 2 days.

When you are ready to roast the turkey, prepare a roasting pan by rubbing with olive oil. Lay celery pieces in the pan, alternating with rows of apple wedges to form a "roasting rack" for the turkey. Lay rosemary sprigs on top of the "roasting rack."

Remove the turkey breast from the brine; discard brine. Position the breast on top of the "roasting rack." Leave the turkey on the counter for 20–30 minutes before putting it in the oven. Preheat oven to 350 degrees.

Roast the turkey for 30 minutes, then brush with 1 tablespoon olive oil. Continue roasting, basting once or twice with the drippings, for about 20 to 30 minutes longer, or until an instant-read thermometer inserted into the thickest part of the meat, away from the bone, registers 160 degrees. Keep tabs on the temperature, as brined turkey tends to cook faster than unbrined. Remove from the oven, tent loosely with aluminum foil, and let rest for 30 minutes (the meat will continue to cook).

Tips for the cook

- If preparing turkey on a preheated gas or charcoal grill, position a disposable aluminum pan under the rack where the turkey will be placed. Add an inch of water to the pan along with celery pieces, apple wedges, and rosemary sprigs. The pan will catch drippings from the turkey, and the celery, apple, and rosemary will add flavor as the turkey cooks on the closed grill. Cook turkey following recipe instructions.

- Most brining solutions call for coarse kosher salt. If you will be substituting table salt, use only half the amount called for in the recipe.

- Disposable brining bags are available at many cookware stores. Plastic roasting bags, found near the plastic wrap and foil in the grocery store, can be doubled up for leak protection and, once filled with turkey brine, can be placed in a sturdy pot or bowl to be stored in the refrigerator.

- This brine also lends wonderful flavor to thick pork chops or a pork roast. ◊

GLAZED HONEY-MUSTARD PORK TENDERLOIN SLIDERS

These sandwiches, built on small buns sometimes referred to as dollar-size buns, cocktail buns, or three-quarter buns, are just right for serving at tailgating fests, picnics, and football parties in front of the TV. Lean pork tenderloin bathes in a mixture of garlic, fresh herbs, honey, and onions before cooking on an outdoor grill. A honey-mustard glaze is brushed over the meat as it cooks. Once the juicy meat is sliced, it goes into buns that have been slathered with Avocado-Garlic Spread and then piled high with Swiss cheese, red onion slices, and fresh greens. Assemble everything before gathering with friends. A bamboo pick works well to hold the palm-sized sandwiches together. **MAKES 12 SLIDERS**

2 pounds pork tenderloin

MARINADE

1 cup thinly sliced onion

⅓ cup water

grated zest and juice from 1 lime (about 3 tablespoons juice)

1 tablespoon minced fresh basil (see tip)

1 tablespoon minced fresh thyme (see tip)

¼ cup honey

2 tablespoons olive oil

2 chubby cloves garlic, crushed

GLAZE

2 tablespoons honey

2 tablespoons olive oil

1 tablespoon soy sauce

1 tablespoon Dijon mustard

1 chubby clove garlic, minced

AVOCADO-GARLIC SPREAD

2 firm, ripe avocados

2 teaspoons garlic powder

2 heaping tablespoons minced fresh basil

2 teaspoons lime juice

salt and black pepper

12 small sandwich buns

Swiss cheese, sliced thin

sliced red onion

fresh greens such as spinach, Bibb, or leaf lettuce

....

Place pork tenderloins on a work surface. Using a small, sharp knife, remove the silver skin, which is the thin, shiny membrane that runs along the surface of the meat. Use a meat fork to poke holes all over the meat. Place pork tenderloins in a large zip-top bag and place in a shallow dish. Set aside.

Make marinade by mixing onion, water, lime zest and juice, basil, thyme, ¼ cup honey, 2 tablespoons olive oil, and crushed garlic in a 4-cup glass measure. Carefully pour over the pork tenderloins. Seal bag and store in refrigerator at least 8 hours or overnight.

Make honey-mustard glaze by combining 2 tablespoons honey, 2 tablespoons olive oil, soy sauce, Dijon mustard, and minced garlic in a small bowl. Mix well and set aside.

Prepare grill. Remove tenderloins from marinade (discard marinade) and place on hot grill. Cook pork tenderloins, brushing occasionally with honey-mustard glaze, until meat registers 140 degrees on an instant-read thermometer. Remove meat from grill. Place on a cutting board and tent with aluminum foil. Allow the meat to rest for 5 to 10 minutes, then slice the pork into ¼-inch-thick slices.

Make Avocado-Garlic Spread by mashing avocados with garlic powder, basil, and lime juice. Add salt and pepper to taste.

>>

Assemble sliders. Spread split buns with Avocado-Garlic Spread. Pile on slices of pork tenderloin, cheese, red onion, and fresh greens. Top with remaining half of bun.

Tips for the cook

- The use of fresh basil and thyme will impart the best flavor to the marinade. If you must resort to dried herbs, use 1 teaspoon of each and give them a pinch as you sprinkle them into the marinade. The pinch releases some of the flavorful oils from the dried herbs.

- Try the Avocado-Garlic Spread rolled into a wrap filled with fresh veggies and roasted and salted sunflower nuts. ◇

PERUVIAN STEAK SALAD

In Peru, there are more than three thousand varieties of potatoes, differing in size, shape, color, texture, and taste, but they all have their place in Peruvian cuisine. This unique salad mixes beef and roasted potatoes with grilled vegetables and fresh greens. Allowing the meat time to lounge in a thick garlic and parsley marinade gives it delicious flavor. The colorful sweet peppers add tangy taste and crunchy texture along with loads of vitamins A and C. And who would think to add chunks of roasted potatoes to a fresh green salad? Potato-loving Peruvians, of course. It's a wonderful surprise.

SERVES 6–8

1½–2 pounds skirt steak or flank steak (see tip)

MARINADE

9 cloves garlic, smashed

½ cup olive oil

2 tablespoons honey

1 cup fresh flat-leaf parsley leaves

3 tablespoons white wine vinegar

1 jalapeño, seeds removed, coarsely chopped

1 teaspoon dried oregano (see tip)

1 teaspoon sweet Hungarian paprika

DRESSING

2 tablespoons minced garlic

1 teaspoon dried oregano (see tip)

½ cup fresh flat-leaf parsley leaves, chopped

¼ cup white wine vinegar

1 teaspoon honey

½ cup olive oil

¼ teaspoon salt

⅛ teaspoon freshly ground black pepper

SALAD

2 large waxy potatoes, such as Yukon Gold
   or red, purple, or French fingerling

olive oil

1 green bell pepper

1 yellow bell pepper

1 red bell pepper

1 large red onion

2 heads romaine lettuce, rinsed and sliced

1 large tomato, cut into bite-size pieces

....

Make marinade by putting all the ingredients into a blender and processing just long enough to mix the ingredients and chop the garlic, parsley, and jalapeño. Place steak in a large zip-top bag and marinate, refrigerated, 8 to 12 hours.

For the dressing, mix garlic, oregano, parsley, vinegar, and honey in a 2-cup glass measure or bowl. Gradually whisk in olive oil. Add salt and pepper. Store in a tightly sealed jar in the refrigerator.

\>\>

Preheat oven to 350 degrees. Rinse potatoes and cut into wedges. Coat wedges lightly with olive oil and place on an aluminum foil–lined baking pan. Bake until tender and browned, 30 to 45 minutes. While potatoes are baking, prepare remaining vegetables. Cut peppers in half and remove seeds and membranes. Cut onion lengthwise into ¼-inch-thick slices.

If using bamboo skewers, soak them in water in a shallow dish for about an hour before grilling time.

Prepare the grill. Gently smash the pepper halves with your hand to flatten them for grilling. Lightly brush peppers and onion with olive oil.

Remove steak from marinade; discard marinade. Sprinkle with a little salt and pepper. Roll up, starting with a long side, to form a log. Cut log into slices about 2 inches wide. Push meat roll-ups onto skewers and set on a platter.

Place peppers and onion directly on grill rack and cook both sides of the vegetables until just tender. Remove from heat and set aside. Place skewers of meat on medium-hot grill and cook for about 6 to 8 minutes on each side, until meat reaches desired doneness. While meat is on the grill, chop peppers and onion. Cut potatoes into bite-size chunks. Toss romaine lettuce, peppers, onion, potatoes, and tomato together in a large salad bowl with enough dressing to lightly coat all the ingredients. Serve steak along with the dressed salad on individual plates.

Tips for the cook

- If you have bee-friendly oregano growing in your garden, use the fresh leaves in the marinade and dressing. A good rule of thumb to consider when using fresh and dried herbs is 1 teaspoon of dried herbs is equal to 1 tablespoon of the fresh variety.

- Ask the butcher at your favorite meat counter to run the skirt or flank steak through the tenderizer once. Skirt steak is my favorite for this salad. ✧

HONEY-KISSED FRIED FISH

I smile when I think of summer days at the lake long ago when my mom pre-pared the little sunnies and crappies brought in by my two little guys and their dad, an inexperienced fisherman. They tasted extra special with the secret ingredient she added—honey. The only times she used this prepara-tion on walleye was when a neighbor did the catching.

For each pound of walleye or panfish fillets:
¼ cup all-purpose or white whole wheat flour
½ teaspoon lemon pepper
1 egg
1 tablespoon honey, plus extra for drizzling
1½ cups crushed saltines
canola oil or peanut oil for frying
sea salt

In a shallow dish, mix flour with lemon pepper. In a shallow bowl, beat egg with honey. Put crushed saltines in another shallow dish.

Rinse fish fillets and pat dry with paper towels. Coat each fillet with flour mixture. Dip into egg and honey mixture, coating fish well. Place in crushed saltines and pat evenly onto fish, coating both sides.

Put enough oil in a heavy skillet to coat the bottom and set over medium-high heat. When oil is hot, fry prepared fish fillets until flaky, about 2 to 3 minutes per side, longer for thicker fillets. Drain fish on paper towels.

Before serving, drizzle each fillet with honey and sprinkle with a little sea salt. ◇

Oven-Roasted Planked Salmon

Several years ago a friend came back from a guided fishing vacation with a new way to cook fish—on a cedar plank. When he prepared salmon for us, he had to go to a lumberyard to get an untreated piece of wood. Now cedar planks are available anywhere grilling supplies are sold. With a fresh, delicate taste and flaky texture, salmon is a healthful meal option packed with omega-3 fatty acids and protein. This salmon takes a brief soak in a liquid infused with Asian flavors and sweetened with honey. It can be served as the main course, used to top a salad, or wedged into a sandwich. **SERVES 6**

¼ cup olive oil

2 tablespoons toasted sesame oil

2 tablespoons rice vinegar

2 tablespoons honey

2 tablespoons tamari

2 cloves garlic, minced

1-inch chunk fresh ginger, peeled and grated

1 (2½–pound) center-cut salmon fillet with skin

2 bunches green onions

1 tablespoon sesame seeds

HONEY GLAZE

¼ cup honey

1 teaspoon toasted sesame oil

1 teaspoon tamari

½ teaspoon grated fresh ginger

½ teaspoon sesame seeds

Preheat oven to 350 degrees. Place cedar plank in the oven to preheat 15 minutes before you are ready to cook the salmon.

While oven is preheating, make marinade by whisking together olive oil, 2 tablespoons sesame oil, rice vinegar, 2 tablespoons honey, 2 tablespoons tamari, garlic, and grated ginger. Place salmon in shallow dish or plastic zip-top bag and pour in the marinade. Allow the salmon to soak in this mixture for up to 30 minutes at room temperature.

Combine honey glaze ingredients and whisk to blend well.

Cut green tops off of green onions and reserve. Remove the cedar plank from the oven. Arrange green tops in a single layer on the plank. Remove salmon from marinade (discard marinade) and lay it on top of the green onion tops, skin-side down. Bake salmon for 30 to 35 minutes. After 15 minutes in the oven, brush some honey glaze over the salmon. Brush more glaze on the salmon every 5 minutes until salmon is opaque and easily flaked with a fork or cooked to your desired doneness (see tip).

While salmon is baking, slice the remaining green onion parts.

Remove salmon from oven and brush with any remaining honey glaze. Sprinkle with 1 tablespoon sesame seeds and green onion slices. Slice salmon and serve.

Tip for the cook The U.S. Food and Drug Administration recommends cooking salmon to an internal temperature of 145 degrees. ◊

Oven-Roasted Planked Salmon

Ratatouille and Rice

This family-friendly one-pot meal goes from stove top to oven and right to the table. It's one of the first hot dishes I make when the air turns cool in early autumn. When you're chilled to the bone, this satisfying dish of wholesome vegetables, protein-rich chickpeas, and nutrient-packed brown rice will warm you right up. Take the leftovers to work the next day and reheat for lunch or pack into a thermos for school lunch bags. **SERVES 6**

¾ cup brown jasmine or brown basmati rice

1 tablespoon olive oil

1 medium onion, diced

2 cloves garlic, minced

1 small eggplant, skin on, cut into ½-inch cubes

1 medium zucchini, skin on, cut into ½-inch cubes

1 red bell pepper, diced

1 green bell pepper, diced

½ teaspoon Hungarian sweet paprika

2 tablespoons honey

salt and freshly ground black pepper

3½ cups pureed fresh tomatoes (about 3 or 4 large) or canned tomatoes

1¼ cups vegetable broth

½ cup white wine or apple cider

1 (15-ounce) can chickpeas, rinsed and drained

1 handful fresh green beans, trimmed and cut into thirds

4 teaspoons chopped fresh marjoram

¼ teaspoon red pepper flakes, optional

2 bay leaves on a wooden pick with a clove of garlic

Preheat oven to 375 degrees. While you are preparing the vegetables, soak rice in a bowl with enough water to cover.

Heat the olive oil in a Dutch oven (or large skillet) over medium-high heat. When the oil is hot and shimmering, add the onion and garlic and stir for 1 minute. Add the eggplant, zucchini, peppers, paprika, and honey. Season lightly with salt and pepper. Cook, stirring frequently, until the vegetables begin to soften, about 5 minutes.

Drain the rice. Add the drained, uncooked rice to the pot and stir for a minute to coat the grains with the oil and vegetables. Add the tomatoes, broth, and white wine or apple cider. Bring to a simmer, scraping the bottom of the pan to incorporate any browned bits.

Stir in the chickpeas, green beans, marjoram, and red pepper flakes (if using). Tuck the wooden pick with bay leaves and garlic into the mixture. If you're using a Dutch oven, put the lid on and put it into the oven. Otherwise, pour everything into a baking dish, cover with aluminum foil, and put it in the oven.

Bake until the rice is barely tender, 45 to 60 minutes. Uncover and let set for a few minutes before serving. Remove and discard wooden pick with bay leaves and garlic.

Tips for the cook

- If you would like meat with this dish, leave out the chickpeas and nestle a roasted or baked chicken breast over each serving.
- Cannellini beans are a nice substitute for chickpeas.
- You can get creative with this recipe. Use your family's favorite vegetables. My husband thanks me when I leave out the green beans. ◇

STIR-FRIES

A stir-fry meal can be quick and easy when you have your sauce made and some chopped vegetables in the refrigerator ready to go. When you purchase fresh vegetables, prep them as soon as you get home from the market. Cut off the florets from cauliflower and broccoli and store them in the refrigerator. Chop peppers and onions. On the weekend, cook enough brown rice for the week ahead. With these steps out of the way, weeknight meals will become healthful fast food for the family. I'm sharing a few of my favorite stir-fry meals that include a flavorful brown sauce, but you'll soon be creating your own mix of vegetables to stir-fry and glaze. Feel free to add meat or tofu to any of these recipes.

STIR-FRY BROWN SAUCE

There is always a jar of this honey-sweetened, Asian-inspired stir-fry sauce in my refrigerator, where it will keep well for a week or two. **MAKES ABOUT ½ CUP**

1 tablespoon toasted sesame oil

¼ cup tamari

1 tablespoon arrowroot powder or cornstarch

2 teaspoons grated fresh ginger

3 tablespoons honey

1 teaspoon Asian chili garlic sauce

In a glass measuring cup or bowl, combine all ingredients, whisking until smooth. Refrigerate in a tightly sealed jar. ◇

STIR-FRIED RICE WITH ASPARAGUS AND RED PEPPER

Asparagus season is short, so I enjoy as much as I can while it's available. This stir-fry is brightened with fresh lemon juice and zest. **SERVES 2–3**

....

1 tablespoon coconut oil

1 tablespoon toasted sesame oil

1 pound asparagus, trimmed and cut diagonally into ½-inch pieces

½ medium yellow onion, chopped

1 medium red bell pepper, chopped

¼ cup Stir-Fry Brown Sauce (page 97)

1 teaspoon grated lemon zest

1 tablespoon freshly squeezed lemon juice

3 cups cooked short-grain brown rice (see tip page 101)

sesame seeds

....

Heat coconut oil and sesame oil in a large skillet or wok over high heat. Add the asparagus, onion, and red pepper and cook for 4 to 5 minutes, stirring frequently. Add Brown Sauce and lemon zest and juice, and cook for another minute. Add the brown rice and cook until heated through. Sprinkle with sesame seeds. ◇

Fried Brown Rice and Cauliflower

In this unique preparation, when you turn cauliflower into little bits that look like rice, cauliflower-challenged members of your family won't even know they are eating it. **SERVES 4**

....

- 1 small head cauliflower
- 1 tablespoon coconut oil
- 1 tablespoon toasted sesame oil
- 1 cup chopped yellow onion
- ½ small serrano pepper, minced
- 3 chubby cloves garlic, minced
- 2–3 cups hot cooked brown rice (see tip page 101)
- ½ cup frozen corn, thawed
- ½ cup frozen peas, thawed
- ¼ cup (or more) Stir-Fry Brown Sauce (page 97)
- salt and freshly ground black pepper
- sesame seeds

....

Remove outer leaves of cauliflower. Separate florets. Put florets in salad spinner. Rinse and spin dry. Grate the florets with a coarse blade in a food processor, yielding about 2½ cups of rice-like cauliflower.

In a wok or a large skillet, heat coconut oil and sesame oil. Add onion and serrano pepper and stir-fry for about 3 minutes. Add the garlic and stir-fry for another minute. Add the grated cauliflower and stir-fry for 3 minutes. Add the cooked brown rice, corn, and peas and stir-fry 1 minute. Add Brown Sauce and cook for another 2 to 3 minutes. Season with salt and pepper to taste. Sprinkle each serving with sesame seeds. ◊

CAST-IRON SKILLET STIR-FRY

At my house, we choose the largest cast-iron skillet we own (12-inch) and use a large grill pan for the cover. If you don't have a large cast-iron skillet, a wok will work just fine. **SERVES 4**

....

coconut oil

toasted sesame oil

14 ounces extra-firm or super-firm tofu, cubed, or 1 pound boneless, skinless chicken, cubed

salt and freshly ground black pepper

1 pound broccoli, cut into florets

1 small red onion, chopped

1 red bell pepper, chopped

1 green bell pepper, chopped

4 cloves garlic, minced

½ teaspoon red pepper flakes, crushed

¼–½ cup Stir-Fry Brown Sauce (page 97)

hot cooked brown rice (see tip)

diced avocado

roasted salted peanuts

2 big handfuls fresh basil leaves, chiffonade (thinly sliced)

....

Preheat the cast-iron skillet over high heat. Place a rimmed baking sheet or a 13x9–inch glass baking dish close by to hold the ingredients as they finish cooking.

Once pan is hot, apply a thin layer of coconut and sesame oils. Add the cubed tofu or chicken and sprinkle with a pinch of salt and fresh black pepper. The ingredients should immediately sizzle when they hit the pan. Cook for about 7 minutes, stirring until the pieces are nicely browned.

Transfer tofu or chicken to the baking dish. Apply a thin layer of oils, toss in broccoli, and stir-fry until broccoli is charred and bright green, about 5 minutes. If you prefer broccoli to be very soft, splash some water over it at this point. Cover the pan and cook for 2 minutes or until broccoli reaches desired tenderness. Transfer broccoli to dish with the tofu or chicken.

Add a thin layer of oils to the pan and add the onion and peppers. Stir-fry for about 3 minutes, until crisp tender. Transfer to the dish with other cooked ingredients.

Add the garlic and red pepper flakes to the cast-iron pan and drizzle with a little more oil. Cook, stirring, until fragrant, no more than a minute, being careful not to burn the garlic. Add the Brown Sauce and mix together until heated through and bubbly.

Add all the vegetables and the tofu or chicken back into the skillet and toss to coat. Season with salt and pepper to taste. Serve hot over brown rice and top with avocado, peanuts, and thin ribbons of basil.

Tip for the cook To cook brown rice, put 1 cup brown rice in a medium saucepan with 2 cups water. If you happen to have five-spice powder in your pantry, add ½ teaspoon to the pot for unusual flavor. Bring to a boil over high heat. Reduce heat to a simmer. Stir rice, cover pot, and cook until rice is tender and has absorbed almost all the water, 30 to 40 minutes. Take pan off heat. Uncover rice and stir to fluff it so that remaining water evaporates and grains separate. Cover pot again and set aside until ready to serve. Yields about 3 cups of cooked rice. ◊

QUICK WAYS WITH HONEY

- Stir 1½ teaspoons grated lemon zest into ⅓ cup of mild honey. Arrange 2 bone-in chicken breasts and 4 bone-in chicken thighs bone-side down in a single layer in a large baking pan. Brush 1 tablespoon of honey mixture over the top of the chicken pieces. Sprinkle with dried herbes de Provence and season liberally with salt and pepper. Bake at 450 degrees. Brush chicken with honey mixture after 15 minutes in the oven and then again 15 minutes later. After that, brush chicken with honey mixture every 5 minutes, until chicken is a beautiful bronze color and the internal temperature is nearly 170 degrees.

- Prepare a luscious glaze for ham by pureeing ½ cup orange marmalade, 2 tablespoons honey, and 1½ teaspoons dry mustard in a blender with ½ cup bourbon whiskey.

- Make a sandwich with thick slices of ham, baked pork tenderloin, or roasted turkey layered with your favorite cheese and honeyed apple slices. To make the apples slices, cut off the top and bottom of 2 small apples. Slice the apple into 4 thick rounds. Use a small spoon to remove the core from each slice. Heat 1 tablespoon butter with 1 teaspoon honey in a large skillet. Fry apple slices about 3 minutes per side, until they are soft and golden brown.

- Marinate a pound of extra-large shrimp for about 45 minutes in a mixture of ¼ cup lemon juice, 2 tablespoons olive oil, 1 tablespoon Dijon mustard, 1 teaspoon honey, 2 minced garlic cloves, and 1½ teaspoons grated lemon zest. Thread shrimp onto skewers and grill until shrimp are pink, about 1½ to 2 minutes per side.

- Serve baked boneless, skinless chicken breasts on rice topped with a honey curry sauce. In a small pan, melt ½ cup (1 stick) butter. Add 1 cup honey, ½ cup mustard, and 2 teaspoons curry powder. Cook and stir until heated through. Spoon hot sauce over chicken and rice.

Glorious Harvest Cupcakes with
Honey Cream Cheese Frosting (page 114) >

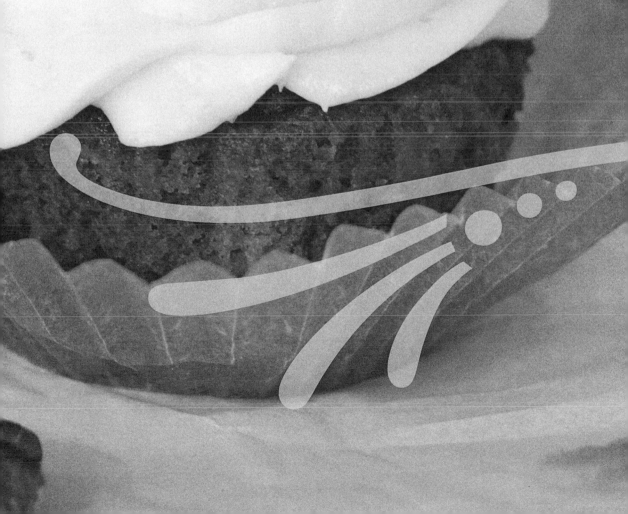

Sweets

L uscious honey is a special treat for everyone who has a penchant for desserts and all things confectionery. Tart rhubarb gets sweetened with honey for a custard-like filling baked over an almond shortbread crust in Rosemary-and-Honey-Infused Rhubarb Dream. It's a dessert you'll look forward to each summer when ruby stems of rhubarb are ready to bring in from the garden.

Gluten-free Almond Cake stays moist with the help of honey in the batter. Its pound cake texture melts in the mouth. Since it does not have a frosted top, it's a perfect candidate for toting to picnics and potlucks. And those who are crazy for frosting, especially when it is made with cream cheese, will be doing cartwheels for Glorious Harvest Cupcakes. These honey-sweetened cupcakes are loaded with carrots, apples, coconut, and pecans and topped with a generous layer of velvety frosting.

Pull your honey jar out of the pantry, dig into these recipes, and start making sweets for your sweeties.

ROSEMARY-AND-HONEY-INFUSED RHUBARB DREAM

A buttery rich crust topped with a luxurious, creamy rhubarb custard is just familiar enough for those who may be skeptical of the combination of rhubarb, rosemary, and honey, yet holds just enough striking uniqueness to interest those with a discerning palate. Serve it with a scoop of premium vanilla ice cream or a slash of whipped cream. Or eat it as is, unadorned and luscious. **SERVES 12–15**

4 cups sliced rhubarb

3 tablespoons honey

1 (6-inch) sprig fresh rosemary, wrapped in cheesecloth

1 cup (2 sticks) butter, softened

⅔ cup confectioners' sugar

1½ cups all-purpose flour, divided

1½ cups almond meal, divided (see tip)

4 eggs

2 cups granulated sugar

1½ teaspoons salt

....

In a mixing bowl, toss rhubarb with honey. Push cheesecloth-wrapped rosemary sprig into the rhubarb. Cover bowl with plastic wrap and refrigerate at least 8 hours or overnight.

When ready to assemble the dessert, preheat oven to 350 degrees. In a large bowl, use an electric mixer to beat butter until creamy and smooth. Add confectioners' sugar and blend. With mixer at low speed, add 1 cup flour and 1 cup almond meal. Beat until dry ingredients are thoroughly blended into butter mixture. Spoon dough into a 13x9–inch glass baking dish. With wet fingers, pat dough evenly into bottom of the dish. Bake for 15 minutes.

While crust is baking, remove cheesecloth-wrapped rosemary from rhubarb and drain rhubarb, reserving the liquid. There will be about 1 cup of liquid. Set rhubarb and liquid aside.

Beat eggs in the same bowl used for mixing the crust. Add granulated sugar and salt and blend well. Add reserved liquid and blend well. With mixer on low speed, mix in remaining ½ cup flour and ½ cup almond meal. Stir in rhubarb. Pour over baked crust and return to oven for 35 minutes, until custard is set and crust is golden brown. Allow to cool before serving.

Tips for the cook

- For a more elegant presentation, cut rounds of Rosemary-and-Honey-Infused Rhubarb Dream with a biscuit or cookie cutter. Coat the cutter very lightly with nonstick cooking spray and the dessert will slide right out.

- Almond meal is very finely ground almonds and is available in all well-stocked grocery stores. ◇

Roasted Honey-Glazed Rhubarb

Roasting rhubarb in the oven brings out its flavor and allows it to hold its shape. A generous amount of honey sweetens the juicy rhubarb as it spends time in the oven. Pomegranate molasses, often used in Middle Eastern cooking, is a thick, slightly sweet syrup that enhances the color of the sauce and adds a sophisticated depth of flavor. This versatile sauce can be enjoyed for breakfast with yogurt and granola and makes a magnificent topping for ice cream, pancakes, and waffles. Or just spoon the chilled sauce into a bowl and enjoy as is—traditional rhubarb sauce with a twist. **MAKES ABOUT 4 CUPS**

- 2 pounds trimmed and rinsed rhubarb, cut into 1-inch pieces (about 7½ cups)
- ¾ cup honey
- ½ cup plus 2 tablespoons pomegranate juice
- 1 teaspoon cornstarch or arrowroot powder
- 3-inch piece vanilla bean, split down center
- 3 tablespoons pomegranate molasses

Preheat oven to 350 degrees. Put rhubarb pieces in a large mixing bowl. Add honey and stir until rhubarb is completely coated. Add ½ cup pomegranate juice and stir. Dissolve cornstarch in remaining 2 tablespoons pomegranate juice. (I do this in a custard cup and use my clean finger to mix it up.) Add the cornstarch mixture to the mixing bowl and stir until it is blended evenly into the rhubarb mixture. Dump rhubarb mixture into a 13x9–inch glass baking dish. Push the split vanilla bean into the mixture.

Bake for about 25 minutes, gently stirring every 10 minutes. Mixture should bubble and begin to thicken slightly, and rhubarb should be very tender. Remove dish from oven. Add pomegranate molasses and gently stir to blend. Allow mixture to cool in dish at room temperature. Store, tightly sealed, in refrigerator.

Tips for the cook

- Add a sprig of fresh lemon thyme to the roasting rhubarb for lovely aroma and flavor.

- Pomegranate molasses is made by heating pomegranate juice to evaporate its water, reduce its volume, and concentrate its sweet and bitter taste and ripe fruity flavor. You can mix the syrupy molasses into cocktails, add it to salad dressings, marinades, sauces, and glazes, or just drizzle it over grilled or roasted meats. It's widely available in grocery stores. ◇

Olive Oil Honey Cake with Honey-Sweetened Berries (page 108)

Olive Oil Honey Cake with Honey-Sweetened Berries

When a friend of mine vacationed in Greece several years ago, she noted the absence of butter on the table at mealtime. In Greece, the land of olive trees, olive oil takes the place of butter. She brought this recipe back for me to try. Olive Oil Honey Cake with Honey-Sweetened Berries is slightly dense, not very sweet, and full of good fats from olive oil and walnuts. Honey and sugar, in small doses, work together to create a cake that is moist and tender. The fresh berries of summer are quite heavenly with this cake. When they are not in season, frozen berries sweetened with honey fill in nicely. Roasted Honey-Glazed Rhubarb (page 106) would also be an excellent mate for this cake. **SERVES 10–12**

....

¾ cup walnut halves and pieces

1½ cups all-purpose flour

2 teaspoons baking powder

⅛ teaspoon salt

3 eggs, room temperature

⅓ cup sugar

⅓ cup plus 2 tablespoons honey, divided

⅓ cup extra-virgin olive oil

1 tablespoon pure vanilla extract

2 cups fresh or frozen mixed berries

confectioners' sugar

sweetened whipped cream

....

Preheat oven to 325 degrees. Cut a piece of parchment paper to fit inside the bottom of a 9-inch cake pan. Grease the bottom of the cake pan with butter. Place parchment round into pan. Grease the parchment paper with butter. Set aside.

Spread walnuts in a single layer on a baking sheet. Toast in oven for 8 minutes. Remove from oven and dump onto a clean kitchen towel. Use the towel to vigorously rub the hot walnuts, removing as much of the tannic, papery skin as possible. Turn the nuts into a fine-mesh sieve, and shake to remove more of the thin skin. It's okay if there is still some skin attached to the nuts. Transfer the nuts to a cutting board. Use a sharp knife to finely chop the nuts. Set aside.

Sift the flour together with the baking powder and salt. Set aside.

With an electric mixer, beat eggs on high speed until light in color, about 2 minutes. Gradually add sugar and continue beating to dissolve sugar. While still beating, add ⅓ cup honey. Beat until mixture is pale and thick, about 4 minutes longer. Reduce the speed to low and mix in the olive oil and vanilla. Add sifted flour mixture and continue to beat on low speed until just blended. Fold the finely chopped walnuts into the batter. Pour the batter into prepared pan and smooth the surface.

Bake for about 25 minutes, until the top springs back when lightly touched and a wooden pick inserted into center of cake comes out clean. Be careful not to leave the cake in the oven too long or it will become dry. Allow the cake to cool in the pan for 10 minutes. Turn the cake out onto a wire rack and allow to cool completely.

Combine berries with remaining 2 tablespoons honey in a bowl. Let stand at room temperature for about 2 hours or in the refrigerator overnight, stirring occasionally. Mash slightly to break down larger berries.

Serve pieces of cake in a shallow pool of berry sauce, dusted with confectioners' sugar and with a puff of sweetened whipped cream on the side. ◊

Almond Cake with Honey Caramel Peaches and Whipped Coconut Cream

Your gluten-free friends will love you for this cake. Bake it in a Swedish almond cake pan if you have one; otherwise, use an 8-inch round cake pan. Either way, this cake has the texture of a moist pound cake that melts in your mouth. Warm Honey Caramel Peaches and a dollop of Whipped Coconut Cream make this a dessert reminiscent of shortcake. **SERVES 8–10**

....

  2 eggs

  6 tablespoons sour cream

  ⅓ cup mild honey

  ½ cup sugar

  ¼ teaspoon almond extract

  1 teaspoon pure vanilla extract

  ½ teaspoon rum flavoring

  1 teaspoon orange liqueur

  ¼ cup almond meal or ground blanched slivered almonds

  1 cup white rice flour, plus extra for dusting the pan

  ⅓ cup potato starch

  2 tablespoons tapioca flour

  ½ teaspoon baking powder

  ¼ teaspoon salt

  ½ cup (1 stick) butter, melted

    Honey Caramel Peaches (page 112)

    Whipped Coconut Cream (page 113)

....

Almond Cake

Preheat oven to 350 degrees. Grease a Swedish almond cake pan or an 8-inch round cake pan with butter. Dust with rice flour and set aside.

Whisk eggs, sour cream, honey, sugar, almond extract, vanilla, rum flavoring, and orange liqueur together in a mixing bowl. In another bowl, mix almond meal together with rice flour, potato starch, tapioca flour, baking powder, and salt. Add to the liquid mixture and stir until dry ingredients have disappeared into the batter. Gently stir in melted butter until well blended. Pour batter into prepared pan.

Bake for 35 to 40 minutes if using Swedish almond cake pan or 25 to 30 minutes if using 8-inch round cake pan, until wooden pick poked into middle of cake comes out clean. Cool in pan for 15 minutes. Turn out onto wire rack and cool completely. When cake is completely cool, wrap tightly in plastic wrap.

To serve, place slice of cake on dessert plate. Top with Honey Caramel Peaches and Whipped Coconut Cream.

>>

Tips for the cook

- If you don't need to make this cake gluten free, use 1¼ cups all-purpose flour to replace the rice flour and the tapioca flour. Leave in the potato starch and the ground almonds.

- If you have a favorite gluten-free baking mix, use 1½ cups of it to replace the rice flour, tapioca flour, and potato starch.

....

HONEY CARAMEL PEACHES

You may decide you want these honey-sweetened peaches in your refrigerator throughout July and August, when the sweet, juicy fruit is available. Spoon the warm fruit sauce over ice cream, pancakes, waffles, or french toast and stir them into your morning bowl of oatmeal.

2 tablespoons butter

2 tablespoons brown sugar

1 tablespoon honey

4 ripe peaches, peeled and sliced

....

In a 10-inch skillet, melt butter over medium-low heat. Add brown sugar and stir until sugar is melted. Remove from heat and stir in honey, blending well. Return to heat. Stir until mixture comes to a hard boil. Add peaches and stir to coat with caramel mixture. Cook until peaches are warm and sauce slightly thickens.

....

WHIPPED COCONUT CREAM

1 (13- to 14-ounce) can full-fat coconut milk,
    refrigerated at least 12 hours before whipping

1 tablespoon honey

1 teaspoon pure vanilla extract

....

Remove can of coconut milk from refrigerator. Open the can and spoon the solid coconut cream at the top of the can into a 4-cup glass measure or glass mixing bowl. Save the remaining liquid in the can for another use. Use an electric mixer to beat the cream until smooth. Add honey and vanilla and beat until cream is thick and fluffy. Use immediately or store, covered, in refrigerator. ◇

GLORIOUS HARVEST CUPCAKES
WITH HONEY CREAM CHEESE FROSTING

When I was in high school, I experimented with a carrot cake recipe loaded with crunchy nuts, sweet pineapple, creamy flaked coconut, and, of course, shredded carrots. I knew I had hit on something special when my mom and dad invited their friends over to taste the cake they thought was out of this world. Several of those friends often asked me to make that carrot cake for them over the years. Glorious Harvest Cupcakes is an adaptation of that special carrot cake. These light and moist little cakes are sweetened with mellow honey and studded with carrots and apples, coconut and pecans. The Honey Cream Cheese Frosting makes them extra special. I'm sure those friends who gathered with my parents to rave over the carrot cake of my high school days would highly approve. Move over, carrot cake—there's a new kid on the block.

MAKES 2 DOZEN CUPCAKES

....

2 cups all-purpose flour

2 teaspoons baking soda

2 teaspoons cinnamon

½ teaspoon salt

3 eggs

1⅓ cups honey

1 cup canola oil or melted coconut oil

2 teaspoons pure vanilla extract

2 cups grated carrot

1 cup grated unpeeled apple

1 cup flaked coconut

1 cup chopped pecans

Honey Cream Cheese Frosting *(recipe follows)*

....

Preheat oven to 325 degrees. Place paper baking cups in 24 cupcake forms.

In a medium bowl, sift flour with baking soda, cinnamon, and salt. Set aside.

In a large mixing bowl, use an electric mixer to beat eggs until light and fluffy. Add honey, oil, and vanilla and beat until well blended. Add sifted dry ingredients to the bowl and blend well. Add carrot and apple and stir to combine. Gently stir in coconut and pecans.

Spoon batter into paper-lined tins. Bake for 25 to 30 minutes, until wooden pick poked into middle of cupcakes comes out clean. Transfer cupcakes to wire racks and allow to cool completely. Frost cooled cupcakes with Honey Cream Cheese Frosting.

....

HONEY CREAM CHEESE FROSTING

- 4 ounces cream cheese, softened
- 6 tablespoons butter, softened
- 1 tablespoon honey
- 1 tablespoon grated orange zest
- 3 cups sifted confectioners' sugar
- 1 teaspoon freshly squeezed lemon juice

....

With an electric mixer, beat cream cheese, butter, honey, and grated orange zest until smooth. Add sifted confectioners' sugar, 1 cup at a time, beating until creamy and smooth. Add lemon juice and beat well. ◈

APPLE CRISP FOR ONE

Children, especially, will enjoy making their own little dish of apple crisp. Everyone will love the sweet fragrance of apples baking with cinnamon and honey.

For each serving:

2 small apples, peeled, cored, and sliced

½ teaspoon freshly squeezed lemon juice

3 tablespoons old-fashioned rolled oats

3 tablespoons white whole wheat flour or all-purpose flour (see tip)

⅛ to ¼ teaspoon cinnamon

pinch salt

2 tablespoons butter or coconut oil

2 tablespoons mild honey

Preheat oven to 375 degrees. Grease individual baking dish lightly with butter or coconut oil.

Toss apple slices with lemon juice. Set aside.

Measure oats, flour, cinnamon, and salt into a small mixing bowl. Use a fork to mix. Add butter or coconut oil and use fork to blend into the dry ingredients. Add honey and mix well. Pile apple slices into prepared baking dish. Drop topping over the apples.

Place the dish on a baking sheet lined with aluminum foil. Bake for 30 to 35 minutes, until apples are tender and juice is bubbling. Remove from oven and allow to cool slightly before eating.

Tip for the cook White whole wheat flour, also called whole white wheat flour, is milled from the hard white wheat berry. It contains the entire wheat berry. The white wheat berry's bran is lighter colored than the hard red wheat berries that produce white all-purpose and whole wheat flour. This creates a sweeter flour. Retaining the bran and germ yields a flour with more fiber and naturally occurring nutrients. Enjoy the mild flavor, the lighter texture, and 100 percent of the nutritional value of traditional whole wheat flour. Find white whole wheat flour in most well-stocked grocery stores and food co-ops. ◊

HONEY-SWEETENED PUMPKIN CHEESECAKE WITH HONEY-MAPLE PECANS AND VANILLA CREAM

At holiday time, there will be no more debates about how to end a meal: pumpkin pie or pecan pie? This creamy dessert combines the best of both. Pumpkin puree mixed with cream cheese and familiar pumpkin pie spices baked atop a crust of pecans, almonds, and oats will please every pumpkin pie fanatic at your table. Sweet and chewy Honey-Maple Pecans fill in nicely for devotees of the nutty pie. A new Thanksgiving tradition, possibly?

SERVES 10–12

CRUST

- ½ cup old-fashioned rolled oats
- ½ cup pecan halves
- ½ cup almond meal
- ½ teaspoon cinnamon
- 3 tablespoons cold butter
- 3 tablespoons honey

>>

FILLING

2 (8-ounce) packages full-fat cream cheese, softened

⅓ cup honey

1 (15-ounce) can pumpkin puree

3 eggs

¼ cup heavy cream

1½ teaspoons pure vanilla extract

1¼ teaspoons cinnamon

½ teaspoon ground ginger

⅛ teaspoon ground cloves

Honey-Maple Pecans *(recipe follows)*

Vanilla Cream *(recipe follows)*

....

Preheat oven to 325 degrees. In a food processor, whirl oats and pecans until coarse crumbs are formed. Add almond meal, cinnamon, and butter. Pulse until butter is mixed well into the nut mixture. Add honey and pulse until mixture comes together. It will be like sticky cookie dough. Press mixture evenly into the bottom of a 9- or 10-inch springform pan. Rubbing a little butter on your clean fingers will prevent sticking. Place pan on a baking sheet. Slide into oven and bake for 10 to 12 minutes, until golden brown around the edges. Remove from oven and set aside.

In a large mixing bowl, use an electric mixer to beat cream cheese with honey until smooth. Add pumpkin and blend. Add eggs, one at a time, beating well after each addition. Mix in heavy cream, vanilla, cinnamon, ginger, and cloves. When mixture is well blended and smooth, pour into prepared crust. Set pan on baking sheet and bake for 55 to 60 minutes, until filling is set around the edges but still soft in the center. Cool on rack at room temperature. When cool, cover the cheesecake and refrigerate at least 8 hours or overnight. Cheesecake can be prepared a day or two before serving.

At serving time, remove cheesecake from refrigerator and allow to warm up a bit at room temperature. Carefully remove sides of pan. Cut into 10 to 12 wedges. Serve each slice of cheesecake with Honey-Maple Pecans and Vanilla Cream.

....

HONEY-MAPLE PECANS

2 tablespoons butter

3 tablespoons honey

2 tablespoons pure maple syrup

2 tablespoons brown sugar

1 cup coarsely chopped pecans

1 teaspoon pure vanilla extract

....

In a small saucepan, combine butter, honey, maple syrup, and brown sugar. Stir over medium heat until sugar dissolves and mixture just starts to bubble. Stir in chopped pecans. Cook gently, stirring, for 3 minutes. Remove from heat. Add vanilla and mix well. Transfer nut mixture to a bowl. This topping can be prepared ahead and stored in a sealed jar or bowl in the refrigerator.

....

VANILLA CREAM

1 pint (2 cups) heavy cream (or what's left after you use ¼ cup for the cheesecake batter)

2 teaspoons pure vanilla extract

2 tablespoons mild honey

....

In a large bowl, beat heavy cream with vanilla and honey until thick and fluffy. ◇

BAKLAVA

This Greek pastry is created with many layers of paper-thin sheets of phyllo dough and finely chopped walnuts and almonds. Once out of the oven, it's drenched with a honey syrup, creating a rich, flaky, sweet, moist dessert. Prepared phyllo dough is available in the freezer case in most grocery stores, and this dessert is much easier to put together than you would think. Your friends will be so impressed that you made it yourself. **MAKES APPROXIMATELY 3 DOZEN PORTIONS**

....

- 1¼ cups sugar, divided
- ¾ cup water
- 2 tablespoons freshly squeezed lemon juice
- 6 whole cloves
- 1 (3-inch) cinnamon stick
- 1 cup honey
- 1 teaspoon ground cinnamon
- ⅛ teaspoon ground cloves
- 2 cups finely chopped or ground walnuts (see tip)
- 2 cups finely chopped or ground slivered almonds (see tip)
- 1 (16-ounce) package prepared phyllo dough, thawed in refrigerator
- 1 cup (2 sticks) butter, melted

....

In a medium saucepan, combine ¾ cup sugar, water, lemon juice, whole cloves, and cinnamon stick. Bring to a boil over medium-high heat. Reduce heat to low and simmer for 15 minutes. Stir in honey and continue to cook just until mixture begins to boil. Remove from heat and allow to cool to room temperature.

In a large bowl, blend remaining ½ cup sugar with ground cinnamon and ground cloves. Add finely chopped nuts and stir to blend.

Preheat oven to 350 degrees. Lightly butter a 13x9–inch glass baking dish. Set aside.

Carefully unroll phyllo sheets and cover with damp towel (see tip). Place one sheet of dough in bottom of prepared dish, folding edges in to fit if necessary. Brush lightly with melted butter. Top with 3 more sheets of dough, buttering each one and folding in the edges. Sprinkle with ½ cup of nut mixture. Top with 2 more sheets of dough, buttering each one as you layer them. Sprinkle with ⅓ cup nut mixture. Continue layering 2 sheets of phyllo, buttering each one, and ⅓ cup nut mixture until all of the nut mixture is used. End with phyllo. You may not need the whole box of phyllo. Just wrap it back up and seal it tightly in a plastic zip-top freezer bag and store in the freezer for another time.

With a sharp knife, carefully cut parallel, diagonal lines about 1½ inches apart and ½ inch deep. Then cut parallel diagonal lines in the opposite direction.

Bake until golden, about 30 to 35 minutes. Strain the cooled honey syrup and pour evenly over the hot baklava. Allow the baklava to cool to room temperature. Using a sharp knife, cut diamond shapes along scored lines.

Tips for the cook

- Phyllo dough dries out and gets brittle very quickly. That's why it's important to keep it covered with a clean, damp cloth. Don't worry about tears or holes that may occur as you pick up the thin sheets. Imperfections are not one bit noticeable in the final product. ◇

Baklava

HEAVENLY HONEY FUDGE BARS

These moist chocolate bars topped with Honey Fudge Frosting are pure decadence. Baking the thick batter in a jelly roll pan means you'll have plenty of bars to share—if you want to. **MAKES 32 BARS**

....

1½ cups (3 sticks) butter, softened

2 cups sugar

⅔ cup honey

1 tablespoon pure vanilla extract

6 eggs

2¼ cups all-purpose flour

¾ cup unsweetened cocoa powder

¾ teaspoon salt

1½ cups chopped walnuts or pecans

Honey Fudge Frosting *(recipe follows)*

....

Preheat oven to 350 degrees. Grease a 15x10–inch jelly roll pan and set aside.

Use an electric mixer to beat butter at medium speed until creamy. Gradually add sugar, beating well. Add honey and vanilla and blend. Add eggs, one at a time, beating well after each addition.

Sift flour, cocoa powder, and salt together. Add to butter mixture, beating at low speed until blended well. Stir in chopped nuts.

Spoon batter into prepared pan. Bake for 25 to 30 minutes or until a wooden pick inserted in center comes out clean. Cool completely in pan on a wire rack. Spread Honey Fudge Frosting on top of bars. Cut into squares.

....

HONEY FUDGE FROSTING

4 tablespoons (½ stick) butter

4 ounces unsweetened chocolate, chopped

2 tablespoons honey

2 cups sifted confectioners' sugar

¼ teaspoon salt

1¼ teaspoons pure vanilla extract

3 tablespoons milk

....

In a medium saucepan, melt butter with unsweetened chocolate. When mixture is smooth, remove from heat. Add honey and stir to melt. Add confectioners' sugar, salt, vanilla, and milk and beat with electric mixer until frosting is smooth. Spread over cooled Heavenly Honey Fudge Bars. ◊

Grandmother's Date Bars 2.0

Every once in a while I daydream about my grandmother's date bars, a sweet date filling sandwiched in a crunchy crust made with loads of butter and brown sugar. This updated version has a crust made of granola, coconut, pecans, and a bit of honey. There's no need to change the sweet date filling with a hint of orange that my grandmother used to make. **MAKES 12 BARS**

½ pound (8 ounces) pitted dates, chopped

¾ cup water

1 tablespoon freshly squeezed orange juice

½ cup shredded coconut

2 cups granola (Honey 'n' Oats Granola on page 55 works great)

1 cup chopped toasted pecans (see tip)

2 tablespoons honey

Preheat oven to 325 degrees. Lightly grease a 9x9–inch baking pan. Line with parchment paper, using enough so that the sides come up over the top of the pan and can be used as handles to pull cooled bars out of the pan.

Put chopped dates in a medium saucepan with water and orange juice. Bring to a boil. Reduce heat and simmer, stirring occasionally, until the mixture is the consistency of a marmalade, about 5 to 7 minutes. Remove from heat. If it is a little chunkier than you would like, pulse a few times in the work bowl of a food processor.

In food processor, grind coconut, granola, and pecans to fine crumbs. Remove 1 cup for topping and set aside. Transfer remaining granola mixture to a mixing bowl. Add honey and mix well with a spoon or your clean fingers until ingredients are thoroughly blended. Dump the granola mixture into prepared parchment-lined pan and press in firmly.

Grandmother's Date Bars 2.0

Spoon date mixture over crust and spread evenly to cover. Sprinkle reserved 1 cup of granola crumb mixture over the top of the date mixture.
Bake for 30 minutes. Allow bars to cool in pan. Carefully pull cooled bars
out of pan, using the excess parchment paper as handles.

Tip for the cook To toast pecans, arrange in a single layer on a baking sheet.
Bake in a preheated 350-degree oven for 8 to 10 minutes, until they are
golden and fragrant. Remove from oven and immediately transfer nuts
to a plate to cool. ◇

PLENTY OF SEEDS BARS

These chewy, honey-sweet bars are just what you need when your tummy starts growling or your energy starts dipping. They're wrapped individually, so you can toss them into your lunch bag, purse, or backpack. They've even been tucked into a cooler and hauled to remote places in Canada as a snack for hungry fishermen. They are quick to make and quick to disappear. **MAKES 2 DOZEN BARS**

1 cup sesame seeds

1 cup sunflower seeds

1 cup coconut flakes

1 cup sliced almonds

1 cup dried fruit (cranberries, cherries, raisins, or apricots), chopped

½ cup coconut oil

½ cup brown sugar

¼ cup honey

¼ teaspoon salt

1 teaspoon pure vanilla extract, optional

Preheat oven to 325 degrees. Lightly grease bottom of a 13x9–inch pan. Line the pan with parchment paper, using enough so the edges come up over the top and can be used as handles to pull cooled bars out of the pan.

Put sesame seeds, sunflower seeds, coconut flakes, almonds, and dried fruit into a large mixing bowl. Stir to mix.

In a small saucepan over medium-low heat, melt coconut oil, brown sugar, honey, and salt together, stirring until brown sugar is dissolved and mixture is smooth. Do not allow the mixture to boil. Off heat, stir in vanilla (if using).

Pour honey mixture over seed mixture and stir well to coat all of the ingredients. Pat mixture into prepared pan and slide into oven. After 10 minutes, stir the mixture and pat tightly back down into pan. Bake for an additional 10 to 15 minutes. When coconut is golden and the top of the bars is beginning to turn brown, remove from oven. Allow to cool in pan.

When bars are cool, pull out of the pan and place on work surface. Cut into 24 bars. Store in zip-top bags or wrap each one in plastic wrap. ◇

UNBELIEVABLE HONEY PEANUT BUTTER COOKIES

Years ago, when my older son was a preschooler, one of his classmates came to our house for a playdate. She arrived with a small plastic bowl of cookies to share with us. The little peanut butter cookies were delicious. When I asked her mom for the recipe, I was surprised to discover the bite-size wonders were made with just three ingredients: peanut butter, sugar, and an egg. Unbelievable. I've added honey to the recipe, resulting in a thin cookie that is sweet, chewy—and still unbelievable. Many will appreciate that these cookies are also gluten free. **MAKES ABOUT 2 DOZEN COOKIES**

1 cup creamy peanut butter
½ cup honey
⅓ cup sugar
1 egg

Preheat oven to 325 degrees. Line 2 baking sheets with parchment paper.

Use an electric mixer to blend the peanut butter, honey, sugar, and egg in a large mixing bowl. Allow the mixture to sit for 20 minutes. Using a tablespoon, drop cookie dough onto prepared baking sheets, leaving 2 inches between each. Bake for 10 to 12 minutes. Cool for a few minutes on baking sheets before transferring to wire rack to cool completely.

Tip for the cook Unlike most cookie dough, this mixture will be very sticky. Don't be tempted to add flour. ◇

GREEN SCENE NO-BAKE ENERGY BITES

When the peanut butter monster in my house decided he couldn't live without some of these no-bake energy bites in the refrigerator at all times, I made a plea for the recipe to the kind people at Green Scene organic market in Walker, Minnesota. Lucky for me, they were happy to share the recipe. They are willing to share it with you, too. **MAKES 24 BITES**

- 1 cup old-fashioned rolled oats
- ½ cup peanut butter
- ⅓ cup honey
- 1 teaspoon pure vanilla extract
- 1 cup coconut flakes
- ½ cup ground flaxseeds
- ½ cup semisweet chocolate mini-morsels

Using a strong spoon and some muscle, mix together all ingredients in a medium bowl until thoroughly blended. Let mixture chill in refrigerator for 30 minutes. Roll into 24 balls. Store in an airtight container and keep refrigerated for up to 1 week. ◇

Green Scene No-Bake Energy Bites

CHOCOLATE-FLECKED COCONUT HONEY ICE CREAM

I'm certain my love for ice cream began in the ice cream shop my grandma took me to when I was a little girl visiting her in Chicago. When my grandma died, my dad continued to nurture my penchant for ice cream with regular visits to a neighborhood Bridgeman's and with his own homemade vanilla ice cream. This honey-sweetened frozen treat is so creamy you won't miss the sugar and the dairy one bit. Small shards of crunchy chocolate are formed when melted chocolate and coconut oil are drizzled into the ice cream near the end of the freezing process. Don't hesitate to leave out the chocolate and add fruit, coconut flakes, or chopped almonds. Personally, I would never leave out the chocolate shards. **MAKES 4–6 SERVINGS**

- 2 tablespoons coconut oil
- 3 tablespoons semisweet chocolate morsels
- 1 (13- to 14-ounce) can full-fat coconut milk
- 1 tablespoon pure vanilla extract
- ¼ cup honey

In a small saucepan over low heat, melt coconut oil and chocolate morsels together, stirring until smooth. Transfer to a small bowl and allow to cool while you make the ice cream.

In a medium bowl, use an electric mixer to blend coconut milk, vanilla, and honey. When mixture is smooth, pour into your ice cream maker and follow the manufacturer's instructions to finish the process. Just before the ice cream has reached the final stage, use a spoon to drizzle the melted chocolate mixture into the working ice cream maker. When you've used up all of the chocolate mixture, allow the ice cream maker to run another minute or two. Transfer to another container and freeze the ice cream until you are ready to eat it.

Tip for the cook I have a few ice cream makers always at the ready. For this recipe, I find it easiest to use my Cuisinart ice cream maker. ◊

Peanut Butter and Honey Popcorn

I've been making this popcorn for years, ever since my neighbor brought a big bowl to my front porch one day. Together, we polished off the whole batch. Peanut Butter and Honey Popcorn is not crispy like caramel corn. It's a bit like eating a soft, creamy caramel with some crunch on the inside. Get popping now and mix up a batch of this sweet, chewy, peanut buttery treat.

MAKES ABOUT 4 QUARTS

½ cup yellow popcorn kernels

2 tablespoons canola or coconut oil

salt

1 cup sugar

1 cup honey

1 cup creamy peanut butter

1 teaspoon pure vanilla extract

1 cup roasted, salted peanuts, optional

Heat oven to its lowest temperature, around 150 degrees. Line two baking sheets with waxed paper. Set aside.

In a large pot over high heat, pop popcorn using just enough oil to cover the bottom of the pot, about 2 tablespoons. Transfer popped corn to a large, oven-safe bowl. Sprinkle with salt to taste. Place the bowl of popcorn in the warm oven.

In a medium saucepan, mix sugar and honey. Over medium heat, bring mixture to a boil. Once it starts to boil, set timer for 3 minutes, and continue to stir as mixture bubbles. After 3 minutes, remove pot from heat. Add peanut butter and stir until melted and mixture is smooth. Stir in vanilla.

Remove warm bowl of popcorn from oven. Pour peanut butter syrup over popped corn and mix until all the popcorn is coated. Add peanuts, if desired.

Spread the Peanut Butter and Honey Popcorn on prepared baking sheets and allow to cool. Once cool, store the popcorn in a tightly sealed bowl or tin.

Tip for the cook The warm Peanut Butter and Honey Popcorn can be formed into balls. For each ball, use your lightly buttered hands to shape about 1 cup of popcorn mixture. ◊

QUICK WAYS WITH HONEY

- Make an easy topping for fresh fruit by stirring honey and a little pure vanilla extract into plain yogurt.

- For a refreshing dessert after a heavy meal, rinse and drain 1 pound of seedless grapes. In a small bowl, make a sauce by mixing 1 teaspoon freshly squeezed lemon juice, ¼ cup honey, and 2 tablespoons of your favorite brandy. Pour the sauce over the grapes and refrigerate to chill. Serve in stemmed glasses with a dollop of sour cream. Makes enough for 8 servings.

- Spoon honey over a scoop of quality vanilla ice cream. Sprinkle with roasted and salted sunflower seeds—just like at the Minnesota State Fair.

- To make a sweet, satisfying snack, pop ⅔ cup of popcorn kernels and dump into a large bowl. In a small saucepan, melt ¼ cup butter with 2 tablespoons mild honey. Drizzle over popcorn, tossing to coat evenly. Sprinkle with salt. You'll think you are eating kettle corn.

- A fruit dip to have handy in the refrigerator can be mixed up in no time. Stir 2 tablespoons honey and the grated zest of 1 lime into ½ cup plain yogurt. Mix up a day ahead of serving and store covered in the refrigerator.

Acknowledgments

For my favorite honey and most tolerant taster, Dennis, who never once complained about sticky handles on kitchen cupboards and refrigerator doors while I worked on recipes for this cookbook and who helps me see the sweet side of everything.

Abundant thanks to the invaluable people who were my recipe testers: Ann Johnson, John Cota, Jan Cota, Cori Rude, Helen Danielson, Micky Jensen, Peggy Desizlets, Lorie Sathre, Mary Chernugal, Bobbie Akerlund-Kotas, Mike Finkenbinder, Selena Wille de Galdamez.

Sincere gratitude to the dear people in my life who helped me believe I should and could write a honey cookbook. So I did.

Index